FRANCHISING

A Practical Guide for Franchisors and Franchisees

GW00726828

2000

*For a complete list of Management Books 2000 titles
visit our website on http://www.mb2000.com*

FRANCHISING

A Practical Guide for Franchisors and Franchisees

Iain Maitland

2000

Copyright © Iain Maitland 1991, 2000
All rights reserved. No part of this publication may be reproduced, stored in
a retrieval system, or transmitted in any form or by any means, electronic,
mechanical, photocopying, recording, or otherwise without the prior
permission of the publishers.

First published in Great Britain in 1991 by Mercury Books

This new edition published in 2000 by Management Books 2000 Ltd,
Cowcombe House,
Cowcombe Hill,
Chalford,
Gloucestershire GL6 8HP
Tel: 01285-760722. Fax: 01285-760708
e-mail: MB2000@compuserve.com
web-site: www.mb2000.com

Printed and bound in Great Britain by Biddles, Guildford

This book is sold subject to the condition that it shall not, by way of trade
or otherwise, be lent, resold, hired out, or otherwise circulated without the
publisher's prior consent in any form of binding or cover other than that in
which it is published and without a similar condition including this
condition being imposed upon the subsequent purchaser.

British Library Cataloguing in Publication Data is available

ISBN 1-85252-316-6

To Tracey and Michael

ACKNOWLEDGEMENTS

I gratefully acknowledge the help given to me by the following individuals and organisations, with special thanks to those who kindly allowed me to reproduce their documents within the text:

Simon Wise, Business Services Manager, and Gary Hollaway, British Franchise Association.

Peter Lowe, Franchise Director, Swinton Group Ltd.

Fiona Parkin, Exhibition Manager, Blenheim Exhibitions and Conferences Ltd.

Lesley Penniston, Franchise Manager, Alfred Marks (Franchise) Ltd.

Roy Seaman, Managing Director, Franchise Development Services Ltd.

Graham Mylchreest, Director, Apollo Window Blinds Ltd.

Steve Mills, Franchise Director, Travail Employment Group

CONTENTS

PREFACE

This book is written both for the owners of prospective, new and established ventures who are thinking of expansion and for anyone who is considering self-employment, perhaps for the first time.

'Introducing Franchising' takes an overview of business format franchising – to use the full name – by setting out the basic characteristics of an ethical franchise, outlining the different types available and detailing the ever-changing franchise market.

Part One is for the potential franchisor, although would-be franchisees will also benefit from reading it to appreciate their future partner's viewpoint.

'Franchising: The Benefits and Drawbacks' examines the pros and cons of this trading method for the franchisor.

'Analysing Yourself' enables possible franchisors to look at their teams, assess their business formats, study finances and check objectives to see that they are all well matched to franchising.

'Organising a Franchise' explains how to commission a franchise consultant, prepare a franchise package, join the British Franchise Association and recruit franchisees.

Part Two is aimed at the franchisee-to-be even though imminent franchisors will find it rewarding to learn about the opposite points of view.

'Franchising: The Advantages and Disadvantages' describes the pluses and minuses of a franchise for the franchisee.

'Evaluating Yourself' allows prospective franchisees to appraise their personality, think about their background, consider finances and contemplate goals to make certain that they are completely suitable for franchising.

'Selecting a Franchise' discusses how to shortlist franchise opportunities, obtain franchise prospectuses, meet franchisors and take further advice before reaching the correct decision.

Part Three guides the two partners through their close, commercial marriage on a clear, step-by-step basis.

'Signing the Franchise Agreement' investigates the length and territory, rights and responsibilities and assignment, renewal and termination conditions of a fair, even handed contract.

'Working as a Team' helps both the franchisor and franchisee to fully understand their relationship and explores how to make the most of the partnership.

'Looking Forward' turns to the future, using action checklists to assist the two parties to build towards continued, ongoing success.

Part Four contains the Appendices which make up a wholly comprehensive reference section providing data about national franchise associations, the British Franchise Association and its full members, associates and affiliates, as at the date of publication, and national franchise exhibitions too. Franchise magazines and directories, and the names, addresses and telephone numbers of other useful contacts are also included here.

The book is illustrated and supported throughout by documentary material, as supplied by some of the United Kingdom's leading franchisors and trade associations. Extracts from franchise prospectuses, application forms, a franchise agreement, codes of ethics and so on illuminate and enhance the text at each stage.

1

INTRODUCING FRANCHISING

Franchising involves one party developing a successful business format which is then licensed to another party to set up and run a wholly identical venture in a particular area for a specific period of time. The party granting the licence is known as the franchisor. The licence is called the franchise. The party buying the franchise is referred to as the franchisee.

Whether you are a (prospective) franchisor or a (potential) franchisee, you will initially want to know about the basic characteristics of a franchise, the different types available and the constantly developing market.

The Characteristics of a Franchise

Every ethical franchise has – or certainly should have – a number of clearly identifiable, distinguishing features.

- The business format is comprehensive and complete. The franchisor provides the franchisee with a trading name, image and goodwill, systems and procedures, products and services plus an agreed operating territory for the duration of the franchise which typically lasts for five years and is renewable for a further term.

- It is also an established and proven success, having been tried and tested through one or more franchisor-owned pilot schemes. This (or it is hoped, these) will have operated for at least twelve months in appropriate, commercial conditions as similar as possible to those in which the franchisee will trade.

- The franchisor offers immediate help and advice, fully assisting the franchisee to start the outlet in accordance with the business format. Such assistance might involve researching and picking a suitable territory; looking and negotiating for a commercial property; dealing with planning permission; fitting out premises; arranging finance; supplying equipment and stock; running a local advertising campaign; handling insurance; providing training in the management of business systems and operating procedures.

- The franchisee pays an initial – or front-end – fee to the franchisor which covers the cost of setting up the franchise. This payment may average from perhaps £3,500 to £15,000, ought to be separated from other start-up costs incurred (a premium to buy a lease, stock purchases and so on) and should not be a source of profit for a reputable franchisor.

- The franchisor gives ongoing support and guidance, constantly aiding the franchisee as and where required. Such aid could include passing on universal systems and procedures; watching changing market trends and appraising their likely effects; steadily adjusting and improving the business format; updating and retraining the franchisee; providing general advice and troubleshooting experts; conducting regional and national promotions.

- An operating manual is supplied by the franchisor. This is the blueprint of the business format, setting out in immense and precise detail how the venture must be run. The franchisee is expected to follow its instructions to the letter at all times, and is usually monitored and checked by the franchisor at set intervals to ensure this is being done.

- The franchisee pays a continuing royalty – or management service fee – to the franchisor in return for back-up services. This may be a percentage of turnover net of VAT (perhaps 5 to 15 per cent), a regular fixed sum regardless of turnover, or a mark-up on equipment and stock provided (possibly 10 to 20 per cent). Paid weekly, monthly or even quarterly in arrears, it represents the ethical franchisor's income. There also could be a separate advertising levy – perhaps 1 to 5 per cent of turnover, net of VAT – for local and national campaigns.

- A binding franchise agreement is drawn up and signed by the franchisor and franchisee. This normally specifies the length of the agreement; the territorial arrangements; the franchisor's rights and responsibilities; the franchisee's rights and responsibilities; the arbitration arrangements; the terms and conditions of renewing, assigning and terminating the agreement.

- The franchisor and franchisee are legally independent of each other, owning their own businesses which they are free to sell as and when they want (subject to any contractual obligations that may exist between them). Nevertheless, they are obviously closely linked by the franchise. Ideally, they ought to view their relationship as a long-term commercial marriage with both parties working together for mutual benefits and rewards.

Types of Franchise

There are three types of franchise, (very) loosely categorised according to the amount of money which needs to be invested by the franchisee to establish the franchised operation:

- **a job franchise**
- **a business franchise**
- **an investment franchise.**

A Job Franchise

Typically, this is taken by a person who wants to start and run a small franchised venture alone. Working from a van or at home, the franchisee perhaps delivers goods or offers a specialised service to the trade or public. Capital investment is relatively low, from as little as £5000, with only minimal equipment, limited stock and a vehicle normally having to be purchased. A modest income is usually derived, roughly comparable to what would be earned as an employee in similar employment. In essence, the franchisee is paying for a job.

A wide and diverse range of trading activities and well known names could be gathered up under this heading, including hat hire (*Felicity Hat Hire*); domestic lawn care service (*Greenthumb*); commercial and domestic cleaning (*Servicemaster Ltd*); damp-proofing (*Dampcure/Woodcure 30*); drain cleaning (*Dyno-Rod*); milk deliveries (*Unigate Dairies Ltd*). Addresses and telephone numbers are listed in Appendix B (page 152) and Appendix C (page 159).

A Business Franchise

Popular with husband-and-wife teams or their equivalent, this is a more substantial and costly concern with products and services being sold from commercial premises such as a shop or office. Outlay can be high – from around £30,000 upwards and often in excess of £100,000 – as property, fixtures and fittings, equipment, machinery and stock have to be acquired at considerable expense. Naturally, the financial rewards ought to be greater than those of a job franchise.

A cross-section of different activities and established trading names which could be incorporated within this particular category are same day light haulage (*Mercury Express Ltd.*); fast-food takeaways and deliveries (*Perfect Pizza*); film developing and printing (*Snappy Snaps (UK) plc*); quick printing (*Prontaprint plc*); shop signs (*Fastsigns*). Relevant addresses and telephone numbers are given in Appendix B (page 152).

An Investment Franchise

Most likely to be purchased by a company looking for a long-term return on its investment rather than a regular income, a management team is often installed to actually sell goods and services on a day-to-day basis. Capital expenditure is prohibitive – sometimes reaching above £300,000 – and normally well beyond the resources of most private individuals and couples. In due course, the financial returns should be extremely lucrative.

Various trading activities and respected names with which you may be familiar could be linked together with this type of business format franchise, namely fast-food restaurants *(McDonald's)*; cosmetics and toiletries retailing *(Body Shop)*; self-drive car, van and truck rentals *(Budget Rent-a-Car)*. Addresses and telephone numbers are detailed in Appendix B (page 152) and Appendix C (page 159).

About the Franchise Market

The NatWest/British Franchising Association Franchise Survey 1999 – commissioned by the British Franchise Association (BFA) and sponsored by National Westminster Bank plc – provides a fully comprehensive picture of the franchise market. Its key findings make interesting preliminary background reading for all would-be franchisors and franchisees. Some of the salient points are summerised here.

The number of **franchise systems** – or business formats – rose from around 170 in the mid-1980s to 380 by 1990 and to just under 600 by the time of the 1999 survey. Previous surveys analysed the range of franchise systems under a set of categories that consisted of business services; home improvements; property maintenance; food; health and beauty; fast food; leisure; transport; vehicle maintenance; clothing; print; and convenience retailing. The 1999 survey adopts for the first time the six categories developed by the European Franchise Federation:

- Hotel and catering   97 systems
- Store retailing   91 systems
- Personal services   94 systems
- Property services   111 systems
- Transport and vehicle services   66 systems
- Business and commercial services   130 systems

The comparative percentages of these categories for the 1999 year are shown in the chart below.

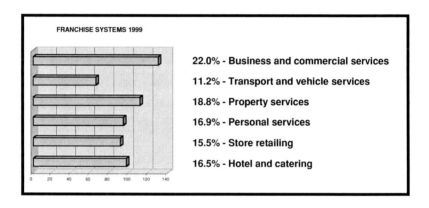

FRANCHISE SYSTEMS 1999

22.0% - **Business and commercial services**

11.2% - **Transport and vehicle services**

18.8% - **Property services**

16.9% - **Personal services**

15.5% - **Store retailing**

16.5% - **Hotel and catering**

Individual franchised units increased from 7,900 in 1984 to 18,620 by 1990 and to some 30,000 by the start of the year 1999, employing around 300,000 people. (Note that the figure of 30,000 includes about 4,500 franchised dairy roundsmen.) The numbers of franchised units and the number of people employed in franchising is steadily increasing year by year. Although some businesses fail, for a variety of reasons, and people leave franchising, overall, franchising continues to attract a steady flow of new entrants which more than adequately compensates for losses.

The numbers of units analysed in the 1999 survey are:

- Hotel and catering   6015 units
- Store retailing   4275 units
- Personal services   4295 units

- Property services   3570 units
- Transport and vehicle services   3105 units
- Business and commercial services 4240 units

The following chart shows the percentages of **franchised units** for the 1999 analysis, divided into the same categories.

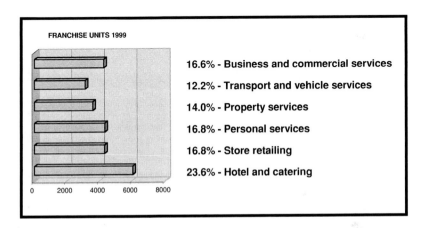

By 1999, about 23 percent of franchisors had interests elsewhere in Europe.

The **gross turnover** of the franchising industry has improved from £0.85 billion in 1984 through £5.24 billion in 1990 and to £7.4bn towards the end of the century. Note that if soft drinks franchises, motor distribution partnerships and tenanted pubs are included, the franchise-related market is worth around £58bn, almost a third of the UK's total retail sales. The franchise market is expected to continue to expand throughout the 2000s and beyond.

Key Facts

All reputable franchises share various common characteristics. Potential franchisors must strive to incorporate these within their planned franchise. Would-be franchisees should look for them in any appealing franchise.

Job, business and investment franchises are available. They may be categorised according to investment levels. They are typified by their franchisees, usually sole traders, partnerships and companies respectively.

The franchise market has grown rapidly in recent years. It will continue to expand in all respects – formats, outlets, turnovers and people employed. Franchising appears to be an attractive proposition for both prospective franchisors and franchisees.

PART ONE:
BEING A FRANCHISOR

2

FRANCHISING: THE BENEFITS AND DRAWBACKS

Whether you're contemplating franchising all or part of your existing concern or developing an idea into a franchisable business format – or even if you are a (prospective) franchisee wanting to understand a franchisor's point of view – you must start by thinking about the benefits and drawbacks of franchising for a franchisor. Prior to investigating the matter any further, you should be sure that there are more positive than negative aspects and this particular course of action is potentially suitable in your individual circumstances.

The Benefits of Franchising

The key benefits of expanding a venture via a network of franchised units – instead of establishing your own outlets – may be broadly classified under these headings:

- **low capital expenditure**
- **personal commitment and motivation**
- **reduced daily involvement.**

Low Capital Expenditure

Once the considerable costs of organising and marketing a franchise system have been incurred by the franchisor, each franchised operation is set up and run using the franchisee's money. It is the franchisee – not the franchisor – who normally pays for any premises, fixtures and fittings, stock and so forth. Even the expenses involved in developing the individual franchise are, or should be, covered by the franchisee's front-end fee and subsequent royalty payments (although these may be modest in the early months or years as every concern takes time to build up).

By fully utilising the franchisee's finances rather than your own, you can effectively grow a highly successful business for a relatively low initial outlay. An ever expanding number of self-funded, franchisee-owned outlets bear your trading name and through royalties, provide you with an increasingly lucrative return on your investment. Without having to put in a large capital sum for each operation, the risk of financial failure is greatly reduced, too. The franchisee carries the responsibility for raising money and making any necessary repayments (but remember that the ethical franchisor will supply active assistance and advice, as and where appropriate).

Removing two of the restraining factors which usually inhibit business growth – limited funds and high risks – should enable you to expand more rapidly through franchising than by starting your own concerns (although a careful and cautious approach to setting up any new enterprise is absolutely essential). You could soon maximise the potential of your business format on a national instead of a local basis, taking advantage of bulk buying facilities and improved payment terms and conditions, negotiating for nationwide sales or service contracts and establishing yourself as a market leader before competitors can (try to) develop a similarly winning system.

Personal Commitment and Motivation

The franchisee invests time, money and dreams in buying the franchise, launching and maintaining the business and becoming a (longed for) self-employed, independent trader. Often, he or she has borrowed funds, is going without luxuries to pay back a loan, and faces bankruptcy if the venture fails. At the same time, the franchisee recognises that a successful, profitable concern will provide a better income and higher living standards. This heady mix of fear and desire means he or she will inevitably be harder working and more dynamic than any manager, however carefully chosen and well treated that person may be.

Accordingly, many of the time consuming and costly head office and branch management difficulties are avoided in the franchisor/ franchisee relationship. The problem of motivating a manager – with a tricky blend of supervision, discipline, targets, commission, perks and so on – is largely removed. Lateness, long lunches, early leaving and prolonged sickness tend to be much reduced as well. Also, a more stable network of outlets is usually created – without the constant aggravation of managers seeking transfers and promotion and the regular upheavals caused by their continual comings and goings.

With all of the franchisee's energies channelled into the business, it normally becomes leaner and stronger than the equivalent concern handled by a manager. Not surprisingly, the franchisee is always seeking ways of cutting costs, eliminating wastage, improving efficiency and increasing turnover. Thus, you will not only receive more substantial royalty payments from likely additional sales but should further find it easier to draw other would-be franchisees into the network, attracted to the current levels of success.

Reduced Daily Involvement

Although the franchisor provides an established business format plus extensive initial and ongoing services, it is the franchisee who is personally responsible for the actual day-to-day running of the venture, controlling stock, managing staff and so forth (albeit adhering to the detailed guidelines set out in the operating manual). As soon as the franchisee has mastered the systems and procedures and settled down, the subsequent daily involvement of the franchisor is minimal – normally just acting as a sounding board or a shoulder to cry on when required.

Reducing the administrative workload, which would otherwise tie up so many manpower and financial resources, allows you to run your business with a compact team, thus minimising your own costs and staff management problems. You can also concentrate on what you do best – attracting and selecting suitable new franchisees, watching and assessing the ever-changing market, evolving the steadily improving business format, and so forth.

The Drawbacks of Franchising

The major drawbacks of franchising for the franchisor when compared with opening self-owned units could be categorised as follows:

- **loss of ownership**
- **low profits**
- **interdependence.**

Loss of Ownership

Even though the franchisor owns the business format and very closely controls the way in which the outlet trades (by means of the operating manual, regular check-ups and – if necessary – a watertight franchise agreement), the concern itself belongs to the franchisee. Therefore, the franchisor/franchisee relationship is markedly different from that of an employer/employee. With a franchise, both parties are equals, each effectively providing the other with a living. They have to work together amicably if they are to be mutually successful.

It can be tricky to maintain such a delicately balanced relationship, especially if you are only familiar with employing managers. You need to adopt a radically new approach – explaining, discussing and suggesting instead of telling and instructing. As the franchisee becomes more experienced and self-confident – inevitably wanting extra information, questioning policies and practices and demanding a larger say in decision making – a breakdown in communication, co-operation and trust may develop unless you can handle him or her with tact and diplomacy.

Without a financial stake in the franchised venture, you will not benefit from its accumulated success when it is finally sold. Moreover, the sale can be a worrying problem as you may not approve of the franchisee's prospective buyer, feeling reluctant to let them join your network. Similarly, if you choose to put your own business on the market, you will be unable to offer many tangible assets such as commercial premises (which could have highly valuable leases should they be in prime locations).

Low Profits

Setting up an ethical franchise often creates early cash-flow difficulties for the franchisor as expenditure constantly precedes income. Organising and marketing a proven format may be costly and carries no guarantee that a franchise network can even be established. Supplying initial and ongoing help – in exchange for a non-profit making front-end fee and slow-to-build royalties – takes money, too. Substantial financial reserves could be required as working capital until a sufficient number of concerns are up and running, all handing over reasonable royalty payments.

Even then, royalties which are based upon a percentage of the franchisee's turnover net of VAT will usually be far smaller than the net profit of that venture (unless direct costs and overheads are unusually high in the individual circumstances). Thus, the franchisor will normally derive a lower income from a franchised outlet than from a self-owned one (albeit for less time and financial investment).

Faced with an initial negative cash flow and reduced money per unit, you may be tempted to cut corners in search of speedier and larger financial gains. This is always counterproductive in the long term, though. Inadequately testing the business format might reduce early outgoings but will almost certainly produce a shaky network operating on a fatally flawed system. Asking for a big up-front fee could recoup expenditure more quickly but will probably dissuade the sensible and cautious potential franchisees whom you most want to apply. Demanding a high royalty rate may maximise immediate income but could cripple the concern, eventually destroying your own livelihood.

An ethical approach is the only true way to achieve real, lasting success in the franchise market. Early money problems are therefore unavoidable, which means you must proceed from a strong financial base ideally with bank support, working steadily through initial losses towards break-even and on to profits once many outlets are established and others are starting to be rapidly cloned. Any riches to be made will be derived in years, certainly not in months.

Interdependence

The franchisor and franchisee are inexorably linked together for the duration of the franchise. The franchisor is relied upon to supply a complete and tested business system, opening and ongoing help and advice, and so on. The franchisee is trusted to follow the system in line with the operating manual, maintain the good name and image of the network and pay over full royalties on time and so forth. If either party fails to honour their responsibilities to the other, the success of the whole network may be put at risk.

Knowing that the franchisee is looking to you to provide and develop a winning formula and continually give accurate and relevant, individual guidance, can be stressful – especially as you are always expected to have the correct answer to each question and the right solution to every problem. Being aware that the franchisee and his or her family are depending on your know-how and skills for their survival can be a strain, too. If you begin to make errors – such as adhering to outdated policies and practices or recruiting unsuitable franchisees who tarnish your reputation – you may bankrupt not only yourself but your franchisees as well.

At the same time, you have to make certain that the franchisees don't ruin you. Your carefully selected franchisees must be competent and motivated enough to work well and hard but not so overly ambitious that they want to take charge or introduce changes to their own outlets. Constantly having to supervise the incapable or rebellious franchisee is time-consuming, costly and likely to create friction. Also, it is difficult to sack an industrious incompetent, and a rebel who is relieved to go may set up in competition against you in the future.

Key Facts

There are numerous major benefits of franchising for the franchisor. Limited financial investment is required to establish a franchised venture. Every franchisee is dedicated to and enthusiastic about his or her enterprise. The franchisor is only minimally involved in the day-to-day running of a franchised concern. In turn, each of these pluses has other, knock-on effects which are in the franchisor's favour.

There are various significant drawbacks. A franchised business is legally and wholly owned by the franchisee. Profits from a franchised outlet are usually lower for the franchisor than with a self-owned unit. The franchisor and franchisee are dependent on one another for their continued success. All of these minuses have more, negative spin-off effects.

3

ANALYSING YOURSELF

Having decided that franchising warrants serious thought, you must now step back and take a long, hard look at your team, your business format, finances and objectives which will hopefully allow you to calculate whether or not you could become a successful franchisor. You should go further with your plans if – and only if – all of the provisional indicators are wholly positive. To plough on regardless of negative findings will almost inevitably result in you and the franchisees wasting your mutually invested time, energy and money.

Looking at Your Team

You and your team need to possess a lengthy and broad-ranging working knowledge of the business world, as franchisees will (rightly) want you to have seen and done everything before, will turn to you whenever difficulties crop up and will anticipate that you will always know what to do, no matter what the problems may be. Preferably, you should therefore already be trading via your own outlets, honing your varied skills and developing your experiences. The novice entrepreneur who has nearly as much to learn as his or her franchisees has little realistic chance of success, with too many first-time errors likely to be made and a lack of confidence rapidly spreading throughout the whole network.

You have to be clearly seen to be totally ethical in your approach to franchising if you are to appeal to quality franchisees and create a sound and respectable chain of franchised concerns. Nowadays, prospective franchisees entering this scrupulously self-regulated field are bombarded with valuable advice from an internationally admired trade association, famous franchisors, high street banks, accountants, solicitors and so on, all of whom are dedicated to upholding franchising's clean image and worthy standards. Thus, non-BFA members are treated with suspicion, un-piloted formats completely ignored, puffed-up promotional brochures read with cynicism, hard sales techniques met with disdain, high front-end and low royalty fees linked with a 'take the money and run' attitude and one-sided franchise agreements rejected on the spot. Only honest and decent franchisors can hope to prosper today.

Your financial stability has to be rock solid should you intend to steadily piece together and expand a network, honour your service commitments and eventually make a satisfactory profit for your efforts. It is vitally important that you fully appraise the probable financial costs and returns from franchising your particular format to see if it will be sufficiently rewarding – not just for you but for would-be franchisees as well. You can guarantee that they will conscientiously inspect and check all of your figures. Read 'Studying Your Finances', page 32.

You and your team must also be whole-heartedly committed to franchising if you are to enjoy a quality relationship with the franchisees and all of their ventures are to be winners, giving you the income levels which you want to achieve. Losing interest after the initial fee has been handed over and subsequently providing patchy, belated and slipshod services and so on, paying more attention to your own outlets and opening them in the choicest locations and so forth, characterise the unenthusiastic (and short-sighted) franchisor who is riding for a fall. Such an approach will have a knock-on effect – franchisee dissatisfaction, unsolved problems, stagnant sales and profits – that will ultimately damage or even destroy your own business.

Assessing Your Business Format

You have to be sure that you offer a format which is an absolutely proven winner, thoroughly tested and refined under the same vigorous and competitive market conditions in which your franchisees will have to trade successfully. No sensible and businesslike would-be franchisee will become involved with an untried and therefore potentially faulty, high-risk system – and you certainly don't want the other, naive and incompetent ones. The basic framework of the format that you are hoping to franchise should ideally exist now, working well in your own units and simply needing some adjustments through assorted pilot schemes to make it appropriate for franchising. Trying to devise a franchisable format from scratch is not a safe and viable option – too many new ventures fail and the remaining ones take time to establish themselves. Even then, they could be unfranchisable anyway.

The business format also has to have some unique selling points which distinguish it from others so that both franchisees and their customers will be attracted to it. A self-explanatory, easy to recall name such as Kwik Strip and Wash'n'Wax, a secret recipe or ingredient as with Coca-Cola or Kentucky Fried Chicken or the way in which products and services are promoted, such as Body Shop's instantly recognisable decor, layout and pervading aroma, could all give your system that competitive edge. Whatever they are, protect the format by applying for patents and registering trade marks and designs where relevant. If you do not, your competitors will soon copy them, which will eventually bite into your sales and profits.

You have to be convinced that your format is complete in every respect since your franchisees will not have the same length, breadth and depth of skills, knowledge and experience that you possess. If your recruitment process is sound (see 'Recruiting Franchisees', page 71) they will have considerable potential, but this will only be transformed into actual achievements if they are provided with a total 'how to start and run this business' package which they can religiously follow. Assuming franchisees know absolutely nothing – and telling them everything, including such basics as stacking shelves, selling and wrapping goods, taking money and giving change properly – is extremely sensible. Otherwise, their weaknesses may not come to light until they are trading, thus damaging your respected name and hard-earned reputation.

It needs to be a relatively simple format too. Your knowhow has to be promptly transferred and clearly understood by these raw franchisees. If systems and procedures are complex and sophisticated, it will be far harder to find sufficiently able and talented recruits and will take longer to train them and build up a network. For this reason, a fast-food restaurant such as *McDonald's* or *Pizza Hut* succeeds in the franchise market whereas a gourmet restaurant would probably fail. One has a simple menu which may be prepared by anyone who adheres to an easy, step-by-step routine, the other has a diverse menu that can only be created by the most talented chef. Simplified decor, layout, fixtures and fittings should also mean that a wider range of commercial properties will meet your selection criteria and will be less costly to adapt to your uses – which will result in a steadily growing chain of franchised outlets.

Your products and services ought to be as well established as the format itself and preferably sold at premium prices so that both you and your franchisees can derive a regular and comfortable income from them. The range offered must not be too narrow nor too wide. Too narrow, and its popularity may be limited only to certain regions and could suddenly fade away. Too wide, and not all of the goods will be universally popular, and carrying slow-moving stock will tie up franchisees' working capital, possibly crippling their concerns. Neither should they be subject to fads or rapidly changing fashions, as a combination of fluctuating sales patterns, high research and development costs and constantly introducing new products and services will create ill feeling towards you from the franchisees and – as important – will increase the prospects of financial difficulties for you all. (If relevant, remember that your goods will also have to be protected from copycat competitors by patents and so forth.)

The market in which your format will operate and where products and services will be sold needs to be substantial and preferably expanding in order that an appropriate number of franchised units can be launched and run at a profit – both individually for each franchisee and as an overall network for your financial benefit. Hopefully, you will know of various sites where your own outlets may do well, which could therefore be equally suitable for your prospective franchisees. Dealing in a high-class market is sometimes a good idea too, so that generous mark-ups can be applied across the board for your mutual gain.

Studying Your Finances

You must be certain that the potential costs of franchising are financially manageable and the returns will be worthwhile. Inevitably, each franchisor's initial and ongoing expenditure and income will differ enormously according to their type of franchise (job, business, investment), the amount of alteration needed to produce a franchisable format (from minor adjustments to major overhaul), the mix of in-house work and professional assistance (perhaps a 50-50 split) and – not least – their approach (number of pilots, degree of experimentation and so on). Nevertheless, having been in business for some time (and if you haven't, franchising isn't for you) it should be possible for you to pull together many estimates, thus creating an accurate overall impression.

This opening assessment of you, your team, finances and objectives will take up considerable in-house time, which could perhaps have been spent on other, more immediately profitable matters. If favourable – and be aware that as a business person, you may be an expert, but as a prospective franchisor you are a novice – you will need to employ a franchise consultant to conduct a feasibility analysis, investigating the same areas but from an unbiased, outside viewpoint. The consultant should then be kept on in an advisory capacity until you have fully established yourself in the franchise market. (See Commissioning a Franchise Consultant, page 36.)

Pilot schemes will have to be launched and operated for a year or more to thoroughly test and adjust the format for franchising. From experience, you should know the approximate establishment costs (such as finding, obtaining, refurbishing and equipping quality premises), running expenses (including rent, rates, wages), sales (with growth rates and trading patterns) and profits (both gross and net) of a new outlet. You will have to build-in the costs of experimenting as well, though – varying decor and the layout of customers' sales space, changing packaging and point of sale material, increasing or decreasing advertising levels and so forth. Their effects on overheads, sales and profits must be taken into account.

Whilst piloting, an encyclopaedic operating manual will have to be drafted out, probably by you and the appropriate team members in close collaboration with your ever-present consultant. It then has to be printed.

A franchise contract – provisionally prepared in much the same way as the manual – must be finalised by a solicitor who specialises in this particular field. A promotional prospectus needs to be professionally written, designed and then printed in bulk. Refer to 'Preparing a Franchise Package', page 38.

You may wish to become an associate member of the British Franchise Association to take advantage of its many benefits. You will have to market your franchise package, perhaps in national newspapers, magazines, directories and at exhibitions. Picking first-class franchisees – sending out prospectuses and application forms, reading replies, rejecting unsuitable candidates and meeting potentially suitable ones – all takes time, money and expertise. Check out Joining the BFA, page 52, followed by Recruiting Franchisees, page 74.

The expenses involved with starting and maintaining a network of franchised units have to be calculated. If you are already running a chain of your own concerns, it should be relatively straightforward to assess these, with some allowances being made for the differences between the two types of business. Totting up the costs of supplying your opening and continuing services, and being aware of the likely sales and profit levels of a franchised unit, ought to enable you to work out the (non-profit making) initial fee and the (non-exploitative) royalty fee which should be charged so that both you and your franchisees derive a satisfactory return on your investments. Then you can decide if franchising – especially with its early monetary pressures now revealed – is financially suited to you.

Checking Your Objectives

Concluding your candid self-assessment, you ought to look at your short-, medium- and long-term goals, examining them in relation to franchising. Sketch out all your quantitative targets, typically relating to your product and service range, sales, direct costs and overheads, profits, assets, market share and so on. Following this, draw up a complete list of your qualitative objectives, possibly concerning management authority and control, leadership style, confidentiality and so forth. Make absolutely certain that you and everybody else in your team know exactly where you want to go, how you wish to get there and when you want to arrive.

In turn, study each of your quantitative goals alongside the main benefits and drawbacks of franchising to ascertain not only if they can be reached via this approach but also that it is the most suitable way of achieving them. Managing your own outlets may be more fitting in your individual situation. As an example, your twin objectives of maintaining steady costs whilst still increasing your market share are clearly more compatible with franchising, whereas building up your capital assets for the future sale of your enterprise is obviously better suited to self-ownership.

Then appraise every one of your qualitative targets in exactly the same manner to discover which particular course of action is most appropriate in your circumstances. For example, your continuing goals of trying to run a highly centralised and autocratic business, keeping a distance between owners and managers and working on a strict need-to-know basis, are all reasonable aims with a chain of self-owned units but not for a franchise network, where an almost wholly opposite stance really needs to be adopted if you are to be successful.

Whatever your hopes and ambitions may be – and they will naturally vary according to your own background – you must be totally convinced in your own mind that they can all be best fulfilled through the unique blend of advantages and disadvantages which franchising offers to you. Should they be poorly matched or even incompatible – it would be extremely naive to expect to be able to sustain a positive early cash flow or subsequent huge profits per outlet – then it would be wise to withdraw your interest now, before committing additional time and heavy financial expenditure to an ultimately doomed cause.

Key Facts

The winning franchisor must have extensive, hands-on business experience. Being seen to be completely ethical is important too. He or she should be financially secure. Total commitment to franchising is required as well.

The successful business format has to be proven in all respects. It needs to have distinguishing features. It also has to be comprehensive and simple. A varied selection of established, steady-selling goods should be on offer, perhaps at premium prices. The market ought to be large and expanding, possibly of an exclusive nature.

The costs of and returns from franchising must be financially manageable and worthwhile for the franchisor and all of the franchisees within the network.

The franchisor's quantitative and qualitative objectives should be achievable through franchising, taking account of the various benefits and drawbacks of this trading method.

4

ORGANISING A FRANCHISE

Once your preliminary self-assessment has been completed and you are absolutely certain that you have what it takes to be a winning franchisor, you must then commission a franchise consultant to carry out a professional and independent study of your particular circumstances. A second opinion from a widely experienced and wholly objective outsider will prove invaluable to you, given your subjectivity and limited knowledge and experience in this area. Should these results be equally favourable – and back away if they are not – you can then work in tandem to prepare a franchise package, join the BFA and recruit franchisees, thus launching a successful franchise network.

Commissioning a Franchise Consultant

Some years ago, the Franchise Consultants Association (FCA), a trade organisation, was set up to dedicate itself to establishing and developing ethical business practices within the franchise consultancy field. Presently, this function is performed by the British Franchise Association with their list of affiliates, and the original FCA no longer operates as such. To be listed as a BFA affiliate and retain membership, consultants must have held a senior position for a significant period within a reputable franchising company and subsequently need to adhere to the Association's high standards of conduct and behaviour. A list of such affiliates is given in Appendix D on page 164. Respected BFA affiliates can help both franchisors and franchisees, although most potential franchisees tend to seek assistance from other sources such as a bank manager, accountant or solicitor. For the franchisor, a consultant can usually conduct a comprehensive feasibility study of the business in relation to franchising, creating or suggesting amendments to the format, appraising the probable costs, returns and so forth; set up, monitor and adjust pilot operations; pull together the right mix of ingredients for a franchise package; write and/or advise on operating manuals, franchise agreements and prospectuses; establish franchisee recruitment and selection procedures; and assess the performances of the format, individual outlets and the network, making recommendations where appropriate. With a quality consultant, the list of services available is almost endless. He or she can be a walking, talking franchise encyclopaedia.

To pick the best consultant for you, look for various key criteria. A successful franchising track record is vital, so you can be sure they know what they are doing. Being honest and trustworthy is important too, in order that you can be certain of ethical behaviour – giving impartial advice, maintaining confidentiality, disclosing potentially conflicting interests and so on. As anyone can legally trade under the working title of 'franchise consultant' without training, qualifications or scruples, you ought to approach only those who are affiliated to the British Franchise Association and thus bear the hallmark of success and respectability. See Appendix D, page 164.

Chatting on the telephone or at a face-to-face, no obligations meeting, you must ask about the consultant's past experience to discover how relevant it is to your individual situation. As an example, a consultant who has primarily worked in hotel franchising may be the perfect choice should you be planning to establish a chain of franchised motels but not if you are going to franchise your nappy delivery service. Try to assess the consultant's personality, because you need to feel comfortable with it on a personal level as you will be working closely together, perhaps for several years. That enthusiasm and exuberance which immediately appealed to you may start to irritate and annoy when your relationship deepens.

Check the full range of services on offer to see if they match your requirements. Having been in business for some time, you will be able to perform many duties yourself such as writing an operating manual. Others will be better done by the consultant, typically including the compilation of a prospectus and the marketing of the franchise to possible recruits. Also investigate the costs involved to find out whether they are both competitive and affordable. Your existing contacts may give improved value for certain services, perhaps introducing classier promotional brochures for a lower price. Thrash out exactly what you do and do not want the consultant to do for you.

Always request the names and addresses of other franchisors who are or who have been clients and ask for permission to contact any of them. Get in touch with those who seem to be similar to you in some respect – same type of franchise, work activity and so forth. Question them about the consultant's behaviour and whether it lived up to the high ethical standards expected. Discover if their background experience was a help or a hindrance. Query whether they got on well with each other. See if the services were carried out in a prompt and efficient manner, and represented value for money. Rounding off, ask these referees whether they would use the consultant again. If so, why? If not, why not? Then – make your choice.

Preparing a Franchise Package

Assuming that the consultant's feasibility analysis of you and your team, the format, finances and objectives, is as positive as your own appraisal, you must then work together where necessary to set up a pilot scheme – either redesigning an existing outlet or establishing a completely new operation on a franchised basis. No matter how successful your system appears to be for your own concerns, it still has to be tried, tested and proven for a minimum of twelve months in a franchising environment if you are to produce a winning package that will attract franchisees and create and sustain a sound network. The more pilots, the lengthier the time and the more varied locations that you have, the better the resulting franchise package will tend to be.

Piloting enables you to ruthlessly re-examine the format, spotting and amending flaws, experimenting and making improvements and so on. Typically, your trading name may have to be altered. Perhaps *The Door-to-Door-Pizza Service* would be more memorable as *Speedy Pizzas*. Possibly, your franchise consultant will suggest that new trade marks, logos and slogans are introduced (and registered) to freshen your image in the marketplace. So often, systems and procedures – most noticeably book-keeping and accounting techniques – have to be simplified to work well for novice franchisors. Products and services need to be looked at, jiggling prices up and down, limiting and expanding the range and so forth. Almost inevitably, you will find a few that ought to be dropped, normally because they are too faddy or complex for franchising.

Seeing the format operating at arm's length will also allow you to assess your initial and subsequent services for franchisees. Choosing a location, surveying premises, negotiating for a lease, applying for planning permission, attending to decor, layout and design, raising funds, buying stock, arranging insurance, advertising and promoting, training, continuing product and market research – all these familiar, routine steps that you usually take to launch and maintain a business have to be analysed one after another to decide which must be provided for/carried out under instructions by franchisees, and to ensure that you have the manpower and financial resources to supply your services in a swift and professional manner.

A revised and significantly more relevant blend of services should be developed too. You may conclude that franchisees will experience some difficulties in raising finance and will seek to make arrangements to introduce them to your bank and supply all the necessary financial data. A colleague could help them to complete the appropriate forms. Similarly – often overlooked – you might put together an insurance scheme for franchisees via your usual broker. You hand over the facts and the franchisees are then responsible for completing and returning a proposal form, making payments and so forth.

An *operating manual* has to be compiled during piloting and concluded before franchises are offered to prospective franchisees. Normally hundreds of pages long, it needs to be a detailed but simple guide to starting and running the franchised business; it may then be used throughout training and as a hands-on reference source thereafter so that franchisees know exactly what to do in every conceivable situation.

It is best written by you since you know all the nitty-gritty features and individual quirks of your unique format, although regular references ought to be made to your franchise consultant and other team members to check that it is sufficiently comprehensive and simple.

Write down all of the necessary information below these titles:

The Business – perhaps including its nature, how it is set up, its aims, trading patterns, what is expected of each party

Systems and Procedures – such as opening days and times, insurance requirements, the hiring and firing of staff, respective staff duties, purchasing and pricing policies and procedures, display, point of sale and advertising techniques, the role and operation of equipment and machinery, product and service preparation and quality control, customer complaints policies, accounting and reporting procedures, royalty payment methods

Business Forms – with samples and details of what they are used for, when and how to complete them

Contacts – incorporating a who's who in your organisation plus what they do, and names, addresses and telephone numbers of key outsiders, such as suppliers and service engineers. Make sure that data can be easily removed and replaced as and when you update the format.

A *franchise agreement* now needs to be drafted, ready for would-be franchisees who want to be part of your network. Sensible though it is to sketch out its prospective features – in close liaison with the consultant – it must be drawn up by a solicitor who is thoroughly experienced in the franchise market. This contract is the legal backbone of the franchisor-franchisee relationship and has to be clear and complete in case that relationship deteriorates. Approach one of the solicitors listed in Appendix D (page 164) who are well established in this highly specialised field.

Jot down the particular items which you would like to see within your franchise agreement beneath these headings:

- its *length* – five years-plus so you can both make money

- the *territory* – which should not overlap to avoid competition

- *your respective rights and responsibilities* – pinpointing what you are expected to give to and take from each other

- *terms and conditions* – arbitration, renewal, assignment and termination.

You can then discuss these with your solicitor in due course, who will advise you whether they are fair and reasonable, can translate them into legal language and fill in any other areas that you have missed. Refer to 'Signing the Franchise Agreement' (page 119) for further information.

A *franchise prospectus* ought to evolve as pilot schemes are trading, to be sent out eventually to promote the package to those who have expressed interest in taking a franchise with you. Created by merging the skills and abilities of you, your team and the consultant, it has to fulfil the tricky dual aims of informing and attracting potentially suitable franchisees whilst dissuading unsuitable ones from applying for a franchise. It may achieve these goals by being presentable and precise rather than glossy and superficial, providing a comprehensive and honest impression of what's on offer – covering all areas, separating facts from opinions – and setting out the type of franchisee wanted. Thus, the readers can decide if you are right for them, and vice versa.

Make certain that you bring these topics into it:

- *you* – your business (past, present and future), your team (backgrounds and current roles)

- the *format* – its features, systems and procedures, opening and ongoing services, products and the market, piloting information

- *finances* – initial and royalty fees, profit and loss and cash flow projections (explaining their basics, that they cannot be guaranteed and expert advice should be sought)

- the *franchise agreement* – length, rights and responsibilities, terms and conditions plus a suggestion that professional guidance be taken before signing

- the *network* – number of franchisees, where and when opened, communication methods, expected growth

- *franchisee profile* – personality, background, finances and goals.

Extracts from two franchise prospectuses are reproduced on the following pages with the kind permission of Apollo Window Blinds Ltd and Travail Employment Group. An application form is often put inside a prospectus, too – see Recruiting Franchisees (page 71) for further details.

Once your franchise package – fine-tuned system, perfect mix of services, operating manual, contract and prospectus – has been successfully pieced together, it is sometimes tempting to wind down pilot operations. Careful thought and a discussion with your consultant ought to occur before doing this, though. Apart from their financial potential – given your winning format – you may be wise to keep them running so that you can test new ideas, revised systems and procedures and updated products and services before easing them (if and when proven) into the network itself.

EXTRACTS FROM THE APOLLO PROSPECTUS

THE RETAIL FRANCHISE

Are you wondering what your life will be like as an Apollo franchisee? Here is a brief breakdown on "the life" of an Apollo franchisee.

YOUR BUSINESS

From your retail base, centred within an agreed geographical territory, you will typically employ at least one member of staff to manage the showroom, deal with administrative procedures and look after customers directly. You will spend the majority of your day away from the showroom, dividing your time between following up domestic and commercial business enquiries and generating new "sales leads" through a wide range of marketing activities. You could be taking part in a local exhibition, canvassing on a new housing estate, establishing a relationship with the local conservatory manufacturer or visiting the area's architects, builders and specifiers to tell them about your products.

YOUR BASE

The location of your base will depend on several factors. 'Apollo' the team will conduct an in-depth analysis of your geographical territory, using their expert knowledge to decide on the best location. You could be located in the High Street, or on a good arterial route into the city. There are also the more modern retail "parks", industrial estates or shopping malls.

Your showroom will portray the corporate 'Apollo' image and it will be necessary for you to invest in fitting and equipping it with a full range of 'Apollo' products. In some cases, it will be necessary to secure space for a manufacturing unit. In all cases, 'Apollo' will provide professional advice on leasing arrangements, rental rates and conditions. At all stages of establishing your base, the 'Apollo' team will be at your side to help work out the best deal possible, within your budget limitations.

YOUR FUTURE

How far and how fast your business expands depends on your own abilities and ambitions. 'Apollo' will offer incentives and comprehensive support to your business expectations. By developing the business to its full potential, you will return the effort and investment being made by the company. You can look forward to the following rewards:

• A UK market currently worth £500 million and growing.

• A partnership with a world leader in the window coverings business

• Direct contact with your customers.

• An appreciating asset with undoubted growth potential.

• A good standard of living with unlimited possibilities in the future.

YOU

Success in any business depends hugely on the dynamic qualities of the people involved, and the window blind business is no different. Ask yourself the following questions:

• Are you hungry for success?

• Are you self-motivated with enough drive to make a business thrive and develop?

• Can you be proactive and compete for business in a fierce marketplace?

• Do you have sales experience or a desire to work in a sales and marketing-led business?

• Have you good organisational skills and the ability to cope with a variety of tasks?

• Do you enjoy interacting directly with the public?

A positive response to these questions will lead you to the next step in the process of joining 'Apollo', the leading window blinds retail franchise in the UK.

ESTABLISHING YOUR OPERATION

A good franchise operation must be built on the right foundations, that's why 'Apollo' franchisees benefit from the following services:

• Property specialists experienced in the analysis, selection and siting of retail establishments.

• Training in all aspects of product knowledge, marketing and business management.

• Equipment and extensive sample collections prepared for your use.

• Marketing plan prepared and implemented for your business.

LONG TERM BACK-UP

Advice and support for all areas of your business are available through the full time professionals working in the business. Additionally, experienced Operations Managers operate constantly around the country to provide on-the-spot consultation and advice to all franchisees.

Being part of the Hunter Douglas organisation means new fabrics and product variations are continually being researched and developed. 'Apollo' also maintains contact with fashion and colour consultants in order to keep in touch with ongoing changes in modern fashion and design.

TRAINING

The 'Apollo' Training Programme provides the following in-depth training:

• Up to 10 days start-up training to ensure all new franchisees are confident in all aspects of the business, from administration to product knowledge and selling.

• Up to 26 weeks launch support, to provide extra help in the initial stages of your entry into the business.

• Ongoing training courses and distance-learning packages for you and your staff, to keep you up to date with products and business skills.

• Easy to use training package for your agents.

MARKETING

'Apollo' is a company driven by marketing and sales, that's why so much investment has been made in establishing a strong, dynamic Marketing Team.

The Marketing Team provides the following direct services to each franchisee:

• Professionally written advertising copy and press releases for use in your local newspaper or trade magazines.

• Creative graphic advertisements prepared for use when promoting special prices, sales and seasonal offers.

• Innovative point of sale materials, including fabric samples and pattern books.

- Fully coordinated colour sales literature, including leaflets, stationery and brochures.

- Creative, professional colour photography of the full range of 'Apollo' products.

- Yellow Pages advertising.

The Marketing Team is constantly engaged in promoting 'Apollo' products in many of the top trade furnishing and decoration magazines. Firm contacts have also been established with the most popular magazines in the style-setting home furnishing market. (e.g. Homes and Gardens, House and Garden, House Beautiful, Perfect Home and Home Flair). 'Apollo' products are continually brought to the attention of the public via stunning photographic features in the very best magazines.

The Marketing Team also creates innovative national promotions, designed to grab the public's attention and secure additional business for 'Apollo' by featuring valuable prizes in conjunction with special discounts and offers.

OPERATIONS, TECHNICAL AND SALES MANAGEMENT

Our field management team is strategically based across the U.K. to provide initial support following your training. The Regional Operations Managers have a wealth of experience in the technical, sales, marketing and operational details of running an Apollo showroom. In the past, they have managed the manufacturing unit of Apollo as well as currently operating several of the company outlets. This background has provided them with a wealth of experience in the nuts and bolts details of the window blinds business. New franchisees are always reassured to know they can call on such experience to help them with their day-to-day problems.

JOINING APOLLO - THE FIRST STEPS

1. THE FIRST STEP

No single method of getting into franchising sults everybody, that's why there are two ways of joining 'Apollo':

1. As a standard 'Apollo' franchisee you, can buy into a designated geographic area or town and run a showroom selling a range of window coverings supplied by the 'Apollo' manufacturing unit.

2. A Super Franchise provides the opportunity to operate with an 'Apollo'

"Master Licence", giving the aspiring businessman a larger geographical area and the ability to appoint agents and licensees operating in that area.

The possibility of establishing a manufacturing base is also available through this package.

2. RECRUITMENT

To complement the recruitment initiative, 'Apollo' has established a sophisticated recruitment centre, with an assessment method designed to produce quality candidates. After 29 years in the franchise business, 'Apollo' knows the first step to creating a successful business is to find the right people.

3. FUNDING

The first stumbling block for many new business ideas is finding the necessary financial backing. That's why 'Apollo" has established excellent credentials with all of the leading "franchise" banks. Up to 70% of initial outlay can be made available to the right people and it's the job of the 'Apollo' team to select those candidates. Professional advice and guidance will be given to help you prepare a proper business plan and the appropriate documentation.

4. THE NEXT STEP

The information pack is only an introduction to 'Apollo' and the way the business operates. However if your interest has been aroused the next step is up to you. 'Apollo' would like to know more about you and answer any further questions you may still have. Simply complete the enclosed application form and return it to:

The Franchise Development Manager, Apollo Window Blinds
Hunter Douglas Wholesale Division
10b Parkview Industrial Estate, Hartlepool, Teesside TS25 1PE
Tel 01429 851500   Fax 01429 851501
e-mail: franchising@apollo-blinds.co.uk

The following pages are reproduced with the kind permission of Travail Employment Group, and are taken from their Information Pack which is sent to enquirers.

franchise information

The Franchise

Our franchise enables you to use the Travail Employment Group name and proven business systems. You will benefit from the expertise and knowledge we have acquired over many years. In addition, you will enjoy the extensive staff support and administrative services we provide.

Operating Methods Manual

All franchisees are provided with a copy of this comprehensive Manual which details policies, philosophies and day-to-day systems and procedures. The Manual is updated regularly to keep you abreast of legislation, market changes and ways of exploiting new opportunities.

BS EN ISO 9002 Certification

Third party accreditation of our policies, procedures and administrative documentation certifies that our working practices meet the stringent quality demands of this well known International Standard. Our franchisees can therefore be further re-assured of the quality of our business concept. Your own Travail business will be able to secure ISO 9002 certification at a significantly reduced cost.

British Franchise Association

Our full membership status means franchisees can be assured of our sound financial standing, and that our franchise agreement and package represents a fair and ethical business opportunity.

REC

The Recruitment and Employment Confederation monitor the recruitment industry's practices, ensure professionalism is upheld, lobby government on pertinent issues and provide valuable support and information to the industry. All Travail branches are full members.

franchise information

The Partnership

We are totally committed to the successful growth of our franchise network. Your success and prosperity is ours also.

Temporary Recruitment Services

Employers increasing appreciate the significant financial and strategic advantages of flexible staffing, maintaining a level of permanent staff to cope with normal workloads, and using temporary staff of assist with extra orders, sickness, holidays or special projects. Growth in this sector of the market is assured.

Permanent Recruitment Services

Travail can help employers increase the speed with which suitable people are appointed, as well as increase the number of applicants from whom they can select. There are other distinctive advantages like 'no placement, no fee', our access to candidates companies cannot reach, and the time saving offered through our short listing procedures. These benefits ensure a steady flow of permanent placement business. Our service is a vital means of increasing industry efficiency and profitability. A key factor for every company's future prosperity is the sourcing and selection of the right people. Permanent placement business growth is assured.

In Summary

Flexible staffing and effective staff selection are vital to business success. These are Travail Employment Group's areas of expertise.

When combined with profit-conscious management, continued growth for Travail Employment Group franchisees is realistically assured.

Your Next Step

Whilst you need to be sure we are the right business partners for you, we too must be confident you will complement our network. Formal qualifications or previous recruitment experience are by no means essential. We are looking for people with personal motivation, common sense, enthusiasm and commitment – people who want to succeed.

Like operating any business, running a Travail Employment Group franchise is demanding, occasionally frustrating and always challenging. Done well, it is extremely rewarding.

If you are interested in what you have read, then we feel we should meet. Simply telephone us to arrange a convenient date. Once we have evaluated mutual compatibility, we will ask you to complete our application form. We can then discuss in detail a specific business plan taking into account your location, personal strengths and commercial experience.

We look forward to discussing our proposed partnership further.

Travail
Employment Group

10 KEY FACTS FOR PROSPECTIVE FRANCHISEES

1. We were established in 1977 and commenced franchising in 1985.

2. We currently trade from 49 locations.

3. 36 of the 49 offices are franchised, owned and operated by 18 individual franchised businesses. 5 of our franchisees are multi-site, 1 having 8 offices, 1 having 5 offices, 1 having 4 offices.

4. We own and operate 13 of our own offices.

5. Group turnover for 1998 was £28M.

6. We are full members of the British Franchise Association, our Franchise Director is the Communications Director of the organisation.

7. We are full members of REC, our Group Executive Chairman is an Executive Committee member.

8. We have been nominated as a Franchisor of the Year by the British Franchise Association in four of the last five years, a testimony to our success and ethical approach to franchising.

9. Prospective franchisees will need a minimum of £15,000 unencumbered capital to set up an Travail Employment Group franchise.

10. **Our franchise is an exciting mix of sales, marketing and management, offering the right individuals the potential for an exceptional return on investment.**

Joining the BFA

The British Franchise Association has been described as the voice of franchising, and rightly so. Its highly successful aims are best summarised as the development, recognition and regulation of ethical franchising throughout the United Kingdom and European Community. The Association was formed in 1977 to:

- to develop and continuously improve standards of good practice in franchising
- to accredit franchisors who meet those standards
- to promote good franchising, as represented by accredited franchisors, to the general public, the business community, government and the media
- to provide to the general public, as prospective franchisees, information and education to help them make effective judgements in choosing the best franchise for them.

Franchisors who meet its strict selection and membership criteria can apply to be either **Full** or **Associate** members (for an annual subscription of £1,850 (plus VAT) and £1,750 (plus VAT) respectively at the rates applicable in the year 2000). A **Provisional** listing is also kept for companies new to franchising (at an annual rate of £1,250 (plus VAT)). Skilled professional advisers – accountants, consultants and so on – who operate in the franchise market may be eligible for **Affiliate** membership (at the 2000 rate of £1,850 plus VAT).

To become an associate member – as you should now be able to do – franchisors must be prepared to commit themselves to following the BFA's various and wide ranging codes and procedures, perhaps typified by the European Code of Ethics together with the BFA's Extension and Interpretation document, reproduced on pages 55 to 63. They should also show that their business is viable, producing two years' audited accounts which indicate it is sufficiently profitable to maintain a franchise network. Then, they have to prove the format is franchisable, supplying one year's audited accounts for a pilot franchise which illustrates a trading performance in line with

BRITISH FRANCHISE ASSOCIATION

CODE OF ETHICAL CONDUCT

This Code of Ethical Conduct in franchising takes as its foundation the Code developed by the European Franchise Federation. In adopting the Code, the Federation recognised that national requirements may necessitate certain other clauses or provisions and delegated responsibility for the presentation and implementation of the Code in their own country to individual member National Franchise Associations.

The Extension and Interpretation which follows the European Code has been adopted by the British Franchise Association, and agreed by the European Franchise Federation, for the application of the European Code of Ethics for Franchising by the British Franchise Association within the United Kingdom of Great Britain and Northern Ireland.

EUROPEAN CODE OF ETHICS FOR FRANCHISING

1. DEFINITION OF FRANCHISING

Franchising is a system of marketing goods and/or services and/or technology, which is based upon a close and ongoing collaboration between legally and financially separate and independent undertakings, the Franchisor and its Individual Franchisees, whereby the Franchisor grants its Individual Franchisees the right, and imposes the obligation, to conduct a business in accordance with the Franchisor's concept. The right entitles and compels the individual Franchisee, in exchange for a direct or indirect financial consideration, to use the Franchisor's trade name, and/or trade mark and/or service mark, know-how(*), business and technical methods, procedural system, and other industrial and/or intellectual property rights, supported by continuing provision of commercial and technical assistance, within the framework and for the term of a written franchise agreement, concluded between parties for this purpose.

(*) "Know-how" means a body of non-patented practical information, resulting from experience and testing by the Franchisor, which is secret, substantial and identified;

• "secret", means that the know-how, as a body or in the precise configuration and assembly of its components, is not generally known or easily accessible; it is not limited in the narrow sense that each individual component of the know how should be totally unknown or unobtainable outside the Franchisor's business;

• "substantial" means that the know-how includes information which is of importance for the sale of goods or the provision of services to end users, and in particular for the presentation of goods for sale, the processing of goods in connection with the provision of services, methods of dealing with customers, and administration and financial management; the know-how must be useful for the Franchisee by being capable, at the date of conclusion of the agreement, of improving the competitive position of the Franchisee, in particular by improving the Franchisee's performance or helping it to enter a new market.

• "identified" means that the know-how must be described in a sufficiently comprehensive manner so as to make it possible to verify that it fulfils the criteria of secrecy and substantiality; the description of the know-how can either be set out in the franchise agreement or in a separate document or recorded in any other appropriate form.

2. GUIDING PRINCIPLES

2.1 The Franchisor is the initiator of a franchise network, composed of itself and its Individual Franchisees, of which the Franchisor is the long-term guardian.

2.2   THE OBLIGATIONS OF THE FRANCHISOR:

The Franchisor shall

-    have operated a business concept with success, for a reasonable time and in at least one pilot unit before starting its franchise network;

-    be the owner, or have legal rights to the use, of its network's trade name, trade mark or other distinguishing identification;

-    provide the Individual Franchisee with initial training and continuing commercial and/or technical assistance during the entire life of the agreement.

2.3   THE OBLIGATIONS OF THE INDIVIDUAL FRANCHISEE:

The Individual Franchisee shall

-    devote its best endeavours to the growth of the franchise business and to the maintenance of the common identity and reputation of the franchise network;

- supply the Franchisor with verifiable operating data to facilitate the determination of performance and the financial statements necessary for effective management guidance, and allow the Franchisor, and/or its agents, to have access to the individual Franchisee's premises and records at the Franchisor's request and at reasonable times;

- not disclose to third parties the know-how provided by the franchisor, neither during nor after termination of the agreement.

2.4 THE ONGOING OBLIGATIONS OF BOTH PARTIES:

Parties shall exercise fairness in their dealings with each other. The Franchisor shall give written notice to its Individual Franchisees of any contractual breach and, where appropriate, grant reasonable time to remedy default;

Parties should resolve complaints, grievances and disputes with good faith and goodwill through fair and reasonable direct communication and negotiation;

3. RECRUITMENT, ADVERTISING AND DISCLOSURE

3.1 Advertising for the recruitment of Individual Franchisees shall be free of ambiguity and misleading statements;

3.2 Any publicly available recruitment, advertising and publicity material, containing direct or indirect references to future possible results, figures or earnings to be expected by Individual Franchisees, shall be objective and shall not be misleading;

3.3 In order to allow prospective Individual Franchisees to enter into any binding document with full knowledge, they shall be given a copy of the present Code of Ethics as well as full and accurate written disclosure of all information material to the franchise relationship, within a reasonable time prior to the execution of these binding documents;

3.4 If a Franchisor imposes a Pre-contract on a candidate Individual Franchisee, the following principles should be respected:

- prior to the signing of any pre-contract, the candidate Individual Franchisee should be given written information on its purpose and on any consideration he may be required to pay to the Franchisor to cover the latter's actual expenses, incurred during and with respect to the pre-contract phase; if the Franchise agreement is executed, the said consideration should be reimbursed by the Franchisor or set off against a possible entry fee to be paid by the Individual Franchisee;

- the Pre-contract shall define its term and include a termination clause;

- the Franchisor can impose non-competition and/or secrecy clauses to protect its know-how and identity.

4. SELECTION OF INDIVIDUAL FRANCHISEES

A Franchisor should select and accept as Individual Franchisees only those who, upon reasonable investigation, appear to possess the basic skills, education, personal qualities and financial resources sufficient to carry on the franchised business.

5. THE FRANCHISE AGREEMENT

5.1   The Franchise agreement should comply with the National law, European community law and this Code of Ethics.

5.2   The agreement shall reflect the interests of the members of the franchised network in protecting the Franchisor's industrial and intellectual property rights and in maintaining the common identity and reputation of the franchised network. All agreements and all contractual arrangements in connection with the franchise relationship should be written in or translated by a sworn translator into the official language of the country the Individual Franchisee is established in, and signed agreements shall be given immediately to the Individual Franchisee.

5.3   The Franchise agreement shall set forth without ambiguity, the respective obligations and responsibilities of the parties and all other material terms of the relationship.

5.4   The essential minimum terms of the agreement shall be the following:

- the rights granted to the Franchisor;

- the rights granted to the Individual Franchisee;

- the goods and/or services to be provided to the Individual Franchisee;

- the obligations of the Franchisor;

- the obligations of the Individual Franchisee;

- the terms of payment by the Individual Franchisee;

- the duration of the agreement which should be long enough to allow Individual Franchisees to amortize their initial investments specific to the franchise; the basis for any renewal of the agreement;

- the terms upon which the Individual Franchisee may sell or transfer the franchised business and the Franchisor's possible preemption rights in this respect;

- provisions relevant to the use by the Individual Franchisee of the Franchisor's distinctive signs, trade name, trade mark, service mark, store sign, logo or other distinguishing identification;

- the Franchisor's right to adapt the franchise system to new or changed methods;

- provisions for termination of the agreement;

- provisions for surrendering promptly upon termination of the franchise agreement any tangible and intangible property belonging to the Franchisor or other owner thereof.

6. THE CODE OF ETHICS AND THE MASTER-FRANCHISE SYSTEM

This Code of Ethics shall apply to the relationship between the Franchisor and its Individual Franchisees and equally between the Master Franchisee and its Individual Franchisees. It shall not apply to the relationship between the Franchisor and its Master-Franchees.

BRITISH FRANCHISE ASSOCIATION

CODE OF ETHICAL CONDUCT:
EXTENSION AND INTERPRETATION

This Extension and Interpretation forms an integral part of the Code of Ethical Conduct adopted by the British Franchise Association and to which its members adhere.

APPLICATION

I.   This Code of Ethical Conduct forms part of the membership agreement between the British Franchise Association and its member companies. It does not form any part of the contractual agreement between franchisor and franchisee unless expressly stated to do so by the franchisor in the franchise agreement. Neither should anything in this Code be construed as limiting a Franchisor's right to sell or assign its interest in a franchised business.

DISCLOSURE

2.   The objectivity of recruitment literature (Clause 3.2) refers specifically to publicly available material. It is recognised that in discussing individual business projections with Franchisees, Franchisors are invariably involved in making assumptions which can only be tested by the passage of time.

CONFIDENTIALITY

3.   For the generality of this Code of Ethical Conduct, 'know-how' is taken as being as defined in the European Block exemption to Article 85 of the Treaty of Rome. However, for the purposes of Article 3.4 of the European Code of Ethics it is accepted that franchisors may impose non-competition and secrecy clauses to protect other information and systems where they may be reasonably regarded as material to the operation of the franchise.

CONTRACT LANGUAGE

4.   Franchisors should seek to ensure that they offer

to franchisees contracts in a language in which the franchisee is competent.

CONTRACT TERM

5.   In suggesting in Article 5.4 of the European Code of Ethics that the minimum term for a franchise contract should be the period necessary to amortize those of a franchisee's initial investment which are specific to the franchise, it is recognised:

(a) that for a minority of the largest franchise opportunities amortizing initial investments may not be a primary objective for the franchisee. In such cases the objective should be to adopt a contract period which reasonably balances the interests of the parties to the contract.

(b) that this section could be subject to national laws concerning the restraint of trade and may need to be met through renewal clauses.

CONTRACT RENEWAL

6.   The basis for contract renewal should take into account the length of the original terrn, the extent to which the contract empowers the franchisor to require investments from the franchisee for refurbishment or renovation, and the extent to which the franchisor may vary the terms of a contract on renewal. The overriding objective is to ensure that the franchisee has the opportunity to recover his franchise specific initial and subsequent investments and to exploit the franchised business for as long as the contract persists.

ADOPTION

7.   This Code of Ethical Conduct comprising this Extension and Interpretation and the European Code of Ethics for Franchising was adopted by the British Franchise Association, replacing its previous Code of Ethics on 30th August 1990, subject to a transitional period for full compliance ending 31st December 1991. During the transitional period members of the Association are nonetheless required to comply at least with the Code of Ethics previously in force. In October 1991 the Association agreed with the European Franchise Federation some amendments to the Code agreed in August 1990 and at the same time extended the transitional period to full compliance to 31st December 1992.

APPLICATION FOR MEMBERSHIP

APPLICATION FOR MEMBERSHIP

This Application Form has five parts :

Part 1.   Your description of the franchised business.

Part 2.   The declarations and commitments required by all prospective Members, Full and Associate.

Part 3.   The information required of all prospective Members, Full and Associate, in demonstrating that they meet the Association's requirement that their businesses should be viable, franchisable, ethical and disclosed.

Part 4.   The additional information required of prospective Full Members in demonstrating that their business has a proven trading and franchising record.

Part 5.   General Declaration.

For the purposes of Part 2 of this application you should also have received a document setting out the Codes and Procedures to which you are asked to give your commitment.

Please remember that for the purpose of Part 3 and, if it applies, Part 4, the onus is on you to provide the evidence which shows that you meet the Association's criteria. Please provide whatever information you feel is relevant.

You should have also received with this application form a copy of the Association's Purpose and Objectives. We hope this statement will be developed, as franchising develops, to meet the industry's changing needs. We hope also that you will want to play a part in the development of the Association and its work.

We would like therefore to welcome you to the Association as quickly as possible but we hope you will understand that our name and our purpose depend ultimately on the strength of our standards and the accreditation procedures that support them. Your accreditation may therefore take some time and may involve more than one exchange of correspondence between us. We hope you will bear with us during the course of these essential checks.

Brian Smart

BRIAN SMART : EXECUTIVE DIRECTOR

APPLICATION FOR MEMBERSHIP

PART 1 : COMPANY INFORMATION

To be completed by all applicants

1. Registered Name of Applicant Company _____

2. UK Company Registration Number _____

3. Date Company Established/Incorporated _____

4. Name of Franchise (if different from 1 above) _____

5. Date of first use of the Name (if different from 3 above) _____

6. Names of Registered Directors :

Designation	Name	Date of Appointment
Chairman	_____	_____
Managing Director	_____	_____
_____	_____	_____
_____	_____	_____
_____	_____	_____
_____	_____	_____

7. Director Nominated as BFA Representative _____

8. Telephone Number _____ Fax Number _____

9. Address for Correspondence _____
_____
_____

10. Name of Parent or Holding Company _____

11. Names of Subsidiary Companies _____
_____
_____

12. Nature of Franchised Business _____
_____
_____

13. Do either your Parent, Holding or Subsidiary Companies act as a supplier to your business?
Yes ☐ No ☐

14. Do any of your Directors have an interest in any company that acts as a supplier to your business?
Yes ☐ No ☐

15. Have any of your Directors been convicted for theft or fraud, or been declared bankrupt or been a Director of a company declared bankrupt?
(If so, please enclose separately details of the convictions or declarations and any Certificates of Discharge.)
Yes ☐ No ☐

_____

16. Did your company first operate through company owned outlets?
Yes ☐ No ☐

17. If so, from what date? _____

18. Have you operated a company owned outlet as an 'arms length' pilot scheme for franchising? _____

19. If so, from what date (if different from 16)? _____

20. If not, on what date did you open the original franchised unit? _____

21. Number of company owned outlets operating at present _____

22. Number of company owned outlets achieving expected standard _____

23. Number of franchised outlets operating at present _____

24. Number of franchised outlets achieving expected standard _____

25. How many franchised units do you intend to open:

    in the next 12 months? ☐   in the next 5 years? ☐

26. Please provide the following information (include name and address) : we will be seeking a reference from your Bankers.

    Bankers _____

    Accountants _____

    Auditors _____

    Solicitors _____

    Franchise Consultants (if any) _____

APPLICATION FOR MEMBERSHIP

PART 2 : DECLARATIONS & COMMITMENTS

This section invites you to give a commitment to procedures and codes which may be amended or developed by the Association. Such procedures and codes can only be amended or developed after full consultation with Members, Full and Associate, who, if they do not wish to continue the necessary commitments, will be afforded every opportunity to withdraw from the Association without penalty or disclosure of any kind.

To be completed by all applicants

1. The information provided in and with this application is, to the best of our knowledge, an accurate, full and fair representation of our business.

2. We agree to be bound by the Association's complaints, disputes, conciliation and arbitration procedures and any amendments thereto agreed by the Association.

3. We agree to be bound by the Association's disciplinary and appeals procedures, and to comply with any notices or instructions issued under those procedures and any amendments thereto agreed by the Association.

4. We agree to comply with Association's requirements and conditions for annual re-accreditation and any amendments thereto agreed by the Association.

5. We agree to comply with the Association's Code of Ethical Conduct and any amendments thereto agreed by the Association.

6. We agree to abide by the Advertising Standards Authority's Code of Advertising Practice.

7. We agree that we will not sell, offer for sale, or distribute any product or render any service, or promote the sale or distribution thereof, under any representation or condition (including the use of the name of a 'celebrity') which has the tendency, capacity or effect of misleading or deceiving purchasers or prospective purchasers.

8. We agree that we will not imitate the trademark, trade name, corporate identity, slogan, or other mark or indentification of another franchisor in any manner or form that would have the tendency or capacity to mislead or deceive.

9. We agree to use our best endeavours to adopt best practice in franchising as agreed and published by the Association from time to time.

10. We agree to notify the Association at the earliest possible opportunity of any material change in ownership, direction, financing, or operation of our business.

11. We agree to comply with the Association's request for copies of non-confidential information to be held by the Association, in the case of offer documents and franchise agreements, to be open to inspection by our appointed franchisees.

12. We agree to provide authorised full-time officials of the Association access to but not copies of confidential information reasonably required in accrediting or re-accrediting our company to membership but only on the basis that the conditions of employment of those full-time officials require them to maintain the confidentiality of the information to themselves alone subject on breach to their summary dismissal.

13. We agree to pass on all of our obligations as members of the Association to any Master Franchisee, Sub-Franchisee, Area Franchisee or equivalent licensee that we might appoint.

Signed _____

For and on behalf of _____

Position held _____

Date _____

This section must be signed by the Chairman or Managing Director of the company making the application.

APPLICATION FOR MEMBERSHIP

PART 3 : DEMONSTRATIONS

To be completed by all applicants

1. VIABILITY

You must enclose with this application form evidence that your business is capable of selling its products or service at a profit that will support a franchised network.

The submission of two years' trading accounts together with your audited accounts for the same period showing a business already securing, or capable of meeting a business plan to establish, a well financed and stable operation, would ordinarily be counted as sufficient evidence.

Please list here the documents you are enclosing to demonstrate that your business is viable:

_____

_____

_____

_____

2. FRANCHISABLE

You must enclose with with your application form evidence that you can successfully franchise your operation.

The submission of the business plan for 12 months' trading and the audited accounts for either an arms length company owned pilot franchise, or a fully fledged franchise which show a trading performance at least in line with the business plan will be one part of the evidence ordinarily required here. You will also be expected to demonstrate that you have developed an operating system which enables you to pass on your "know-how" at arms length. You might do this by submitting details of, or providing access to, a copy of your operational manual and by setting out details of the training programme for franchisees.

Please list here the documents (in addition to those provided in demonstrating viability) that you are submitting (or are prepared to give access to - marked "access only'') to show franchisability.

_____

_____

_____

_____

Please also summarise overleaf the costs you incur, on average, prior to, and including opening of, a franchised outlet.

cont/d.........

	£
* Training and manual	_____
* Initial marketing operation including launch	_____
* Goods, material and equipment, if applicable	_____
* Other items - please specify	_____

Please summarise your support to franchisees ie management, technical and training resources

_____

_____

_____

3. ETHICAL

The primary evidence required to show that your business has an ethical foundation is a copy of the franchise agreement currently in use. **Please provide a copy of that agreement with this application.**

We will seek references on your business from a small sample of any franchisees you already have. **Please also include a full list of their names, trading addresses, and the date of acquiring the franchise.**

4. DISCLOSED

You will need to submit with this application copies of all the documents, brochures and particularly financial projections you give to prospective franchisees in advance of their signing a franchise agreement.

Please ensure you enclose copies of your offer documents. £
Please also summarise below the information presented therein :
Cost of Franchise Package to Franchisee _____

Initial franchise fee _____

Franchisee's total investment (including working capital) _____

Management service (or royalty) charge _____

Advertising or Marketing levy _____

Average period to establish franchise on a satisfactory basis _____

Estimated period for franchisee to recover initial investment _____

If you feel able to provide all the information requested in this Part 3 (and you have completed Parts 1 and 2) you are eligible for Associate Membership. As an Associate you will be able to refer to yourself as such (in a prescribed format) on your published material. You will also be eligible for the other services and discounts the Association offers.

If you also feel able to provide the evidence required under Part 4 (following) you will be eligible for Full Membership. If not please complete the general application and declaration (Part 5) at the end of this application.

APPLICATION FOR MEMBERSHIP

PART 4 : FULL MEMBERSHIP

To be completed by Full Member applicants

1. **A PROVEN TRADING RECORD**

You need to provide financial records to show that your franchised network is stable and profitable both for you and your franchisees. Your own audited accounts showing acceptable financial trends over an extended period will be required. We will also need to agree with you a selection of your franchisees from whom we will need to obtain trading accounts. These will be treated confidentially and in the knowledge that franchisees have an obligation to "husband" their accounts.

Please list here the series of your audited accounts enclosed with this application:

_____

_____

_____

_____

Please also provide with this application a complete list of your current franchisees (as also required under Part 3) and nominate below two franchisees from whom trading accounts can be obtained or in respect of which you are able to enclose or submit accounts (we will choose a further small selection of franchisees which we will ask you to approach for trading accounts).

(i) _____

(ii) _____

2. A PROVEN FRANCHISING RECORD

Please provide the following details, in confidence, covering at least two full reporting years:

	Current Year (Months)	Last Year	Year Before
(a) Franchise Starts			
(b) Franchise Failures (forced)			
(c) Franchise Withdrawals (voluntary)			
(d) Franchise Resales from (b)			
(e) Franchise Resales from (c)			
(f) Franchise disputes *			

* Only those disputes which have required intervention (through your solicitor, the franchisee's solicitor, or the Association's conciliation or arbitration schemes should be recorded).

If you have been able to provide the evidence requested in this Part 4 you are eligible for Full Membership of the Association. As a Full Member you will be able to use the Association's logo on your published material. You will also be eligible to vote at the Annual and Special General Meetings, to stand for election to the Association's Council, and to receive all services and discounts which the Association offers.

Please also complete the general declaration (Part 5) at the end of this application.

APPLICATION FOR MEMBERSHIP

PART 5 : GENERAL APPLICATION AND DECLARATION

To be completed by all Applicants

We, the applicant company declare, to the best of our knowledge and belief, that the franchise system we offer is based on sound business principles and provides a viable and ethical business opportunity for the franchisee and a genuine end-product or service for the consumer. It is our belief that the systems we operate, satisfactorily protect both the franchisee and the consumer and, accordingly, we hereby apply for membership of the British Franchise Association.

Signed _____

For and on behalf of _____

Position held _____

Date _____

The Form shall be signed by the Chairman or Managing Director of the company making the application.

CONCLUSION

Thank you for taking the time and trouble to complete this application form. Please do not forget to enclose the documents you have listed, and we have specified, in Parts 3 and 4. We appreciate the complexity of our Membership requirements but we hope you understand that it is essential in protecting the Association's name and standing - without which you would have little reason to join us.

expectations as well as some evidence of a developed operating system to pass on know-how to franchisees. A copy of an operating manual would be ideal.

In addition, would-be associates are expected to demonstrate that they are ethical by submitting their fair and unambiguous franchise agreement, which should wholly conform to the BFA's standards of ethical practice. Furthermore, they must offer proof that they disclose a full and realistic picture of their proposition to franchisees prior to the signing of the franchise agreement. Any documents, brochures, financial projections and relevant miscellaneous material shown or handed over to the franchisees will have to be revealed to the BFA.

To enter as a full member – which you will hopefully be eligible to do in due course – franchisors need to fulfil the same terms and conditions of associate membership and have a franchise network with a proven trading and franchising record. The BFA will want to see details of franchise openings, failures, withdrawals, resales and any disputes that required external intervention – perhaps by solicitors – before they were resolved. Evidence of the profitability of individual franchised concerns and the whole network over a two-year period will also be sought, in the form of audited accounts.

Associates, full members and affiliates (of whom your consultant may be one) benefit from belonging to the Association in many ways. Developing standards for the structure and conduct of franchised businesses, contributing to the development of best practices within franchising, securing an influence on governments and so on are of value to you. Perhaps most important of all, though – especially at this stage – is that it makes you respectable in the eyes of budding franchisees, which will act as a magnet when you want to recruit them.

Write to or telephone the BFA – the address and telephone number are in Appendix A, page 149 – asking for further information about membership. Carefully read the details sent to you, particularly the lengthy and detailed codes and procedures that you need to adhere to. Possibly seek the views of other associate members, seeing how it has affected them (refer to Appendix C, page 159). Should you decide to apply – and it will probably be the best move you ever make – complete and return the application form and your substantiating documents, proving viability and so forth. To discover the exact questions that you will have to answer and to find out about the material which must be submitted, look at the Application for Membership on page 59, reproduced by kind permission of the Association.

Recruiting Franchisees

Still liaising with your consultant – whilst receiving additional assistance from colleagues with practical recruiting experience – you must set out to publicise your franchise package. On request, the BFA distributes some 10,000 copies of its membership lists each year to prospective franchisees, which will often generate sufficient enquiries for you. The full list is also available on the BFA website at www.british-franchise.org.uk. National newspaper and business magazine advertisements (albeit costly) and free articles – sparked off by press releases – may be advantageous, should you be planning nationwide expansion. Similarly, local newspapers and magazines could be an attractive proposition if you are focusing on certain areas. In the early 1990s, for instance, Dairy Crest recruited most of its milk round franchisees for Essex and Suffolk via the regional press.

Read by active, would-be franchisees, specialist franchise magazines and directories such as Franchise World and The Business Franchise Directory are worth consideration (see Appendix G, page 174). It may be beneficial to participate in franchise exhibitions such as the British Franchise Exhibition that takes place usually in January at G-Mex in Manchester, or the British and International Franchise Exhibition in London in April. Details of these and other exhibitions, both in the UK and elsewhere can be acquired from the BFA.

Word-of-mouth promotion – from the consultant and the bank and insurance company through which you have arranged franchisee schemes – is a bonus. Of course, having a chain of well-run franchised operations successfully trading is the biggest and best advertisement of all. With the burgeoning Internet and more companies and organisations (even smaller ones) having their own web site, a wealth of information is now available for potential entrepreneurs.

If sufficient franchise data is always given in listings, advertisements and features – its type, activities, costs and so on – readers should be able to decide if it appears to be suited to them and only a compact pool of potentially satisfactory franchisees will ask for more information. In response to these enquiries, you should forward your franchise prospectus, usually enclosing an application form. Hopefully, the prospectus will explain the franchise package in greater detail (refer to Preparing a Franchise Package, page 38) and those people who feel you are right for each other will apply for a franchise. Expect to hear from perhaps one in every twenty who were sent a prospectus – a good sign which shows that the other nineteen have effectively eliminated themselves, saving you the time and money involved with rejecting them.

Your application form, if it is to allow you to shortlist applicants properly, should seek information on most (or even all) of these topics, as appropriate:

Personal Details – name, address, telephone number, home rental or ownership, time spent living there with previous address if less than three years, status, age, partner and dependents' data, car and clean licence possession, education, qualifications, health, leisure interests

Employment – up to a ten-year history, employers, activities, products and services, positions and duties, salaries, reasons for leaving

Finances – a financial history including bank account and credit cards ownership, credit refusal, bankruptcy details plus investment available, sum borrowed and its source

Other Information – attributes believed to be important, reasons for applying and ambitions, two referees, where the applicant learned of the franchise, additional comments.

Two franchise application/enquiry forms are reproduced on pages 80 and 84, by kind courtesy of Apollo Window Blinds Limited and Travail Employment Group Ltd.

On receipt of completed application forms, you will need to think further about the type of people you wish to recruit. With regard to their personality, you will probably want to see they possess an independent spirit so that they can run their business themselves without referring every minor hiccup to you.

Some signs of administrative and organisational abilities, gained in a work or leisure environment, may be desirable. Having sufficient self-control to adhere to rigid guidelines and not to attempt to stamp their own image on the system is important. Looking for previous work experience and promotions within a restrictive organisational structure could be a good idea.

An ambition to succeed will make them work hard to do well with your franchise, also benefiting you. Comments about purchasing other franchises from you in the future may be a plus point, as long as these are laced with realism.

Mixability is a significant factor so that they can get on with customers, thus boosting trade. Already dealing with the public in some capacity could be an asset. You need to be sure they are trustworthy too, in order that you can limit check ups and visits to acceptable levels. In due course references should be sought from present and former employers.

Concerning their background, you may be wise to seek evidence that they are familiar with and even well known in the proposed trading area, which could mean they will settle in and develop the enterprise faster than a newcomer might be expected to do. Living or working in the vicinity may be a positive factor. An absence of prior knowledge of the work activities involved is sometimes a blessing in disguise as you will not have to eradicate deep-rooted habits when training them. You could decide to reject the former owners and managers of similar concerns for this reason.

Excellent health is vital if the franchisee is to adapt successfully to the heavy workload and incessant pressures. Asking referees about their sickness record or even requesting a medical report from a GP is therefore extremely sensible. Family backing is essential too, so that they can channel their time and energies into the franchised outlet,

FRANCHISE ENQUIRY FORM

CORPORATE CENTRE
74 Southgate Street
Gloucester
GL1 2DP

T: 01452 420700
F: 01452 303197
E: cc@travail.co.uk
W: www.travail.co.uk

Desired Location(s):_____

PERSONAL DETAILS: ❑ Mr ❑ Mrs ❑ Miss ❑ Ms

Surname:_____

Forename(s):_____

Age:_____Date of Birth:_____

Marital Status:_____

Address:_____

_____

_____Postcode:_____

Telephone Number: Home:_____

Business:_____

Number of Children:_____Ages:_____

Car Owner? ❑ YES ❑ NO

Make and Year:_____

Do you hold a full UK Driver's Licence? ❑ YES ❑ NO

Any other licences (please specify):_____

Will your Partner be involved in the business? ❑ YES ❑ NO

If Yes, in what way(s):_____

_____

_____

COMMERCIAL

INDUSTRIAL

SKILLED

DRIVING

CATERING

TECHNICAL

EXECUTIVE

Travail Employment Group Ltd   T/A Travail Employment Group   Registered in UK No. 1334461

EMPLOYMENT HISTORY:

Are you currently:　☐ Employed　　☐ Self-Employed　　☐ Unemployed

Please give details of your present/most recent employment: -

1)　　Company Name:_____

　　　Address:_____

　　　Nature of Business:_____

　　　Employed From:_____To:_____

　　　Position Held:_____

　　　Duties and Responsibilities:_____

　　　_____

　　　_____

　　　Notable Achievements:_____

　　　_____

PREVIOUS EMPLOYMENT:

2)　　Company Name:_____

　　　Address:_____

　　　Nature of Business:_____

　　　Employed From:_____To:_____

　　　Position Held:_____

　　　Duties and Responsibilities:_____

　　　_____

　　　_____

　　　Notable Achievements:_____

　　　_____

PREVIOUS EMPLOYMENT (contd):

2)   Company Name:_____

        Address:_____

        Nature of Business:_____

        Employed From:_____To:_____

        Position Held:_____

        Duties and Responsibilities:_____

        _____

        _____

Please summarise all previous employment experience:_____

_____

_____

EDUCATION:

Please summarise your education:_____

_____

Qualifications:_____

Membership of Professional Organisations/Societies:_____

EXPERIENCE (Please indicate your experience in the following areas):

❏	Recruitment	❏	Interviewing	❏	Advertising
❏	Training	❏	Personnel	❏	Marketing/Promotions
❏	Management	❏	Administration	❏	Exhibitions
❏	Tele-Sales	❏	Secretarial	❏	Creative Writing
❏	Face-to-Face Sales	❏	Book-Keeping	❏	Negotiating

What do you consider your strengths:_____

What do you consider your weaknesses:_____

Greatest personal accomplishment:_____

MEDICAL HISTORY:

Please describe your general state of health:_____

Past Illnesses:_____

Please describe your partner's general state of health:_____

INTERESTS:

Leisure Activities/Hobbies/Special Interests:_____

_____

FINANCIAL DETAILS (Continue on a separate sheet if necessary):

❑ House Owner   ❑ Rented   ❑ Living with Family   ❑ Other

How much capital have you available for this business?:   £_____

Have you ever declared bankruptcy?:   _____

Have you ever been convicted of a criminal offence?:   _____

When do you envisage starting your business?:   _____

What do you foresee as your major problems?:   _____

_____

Have you ever, or are you currently considering any other franchise opportunity?:_____

_____

If so, what?:_____

Why do you think you would make a successful Travail Franchisee?:

_____

REFERENCES:

1)   Name:_____   2)   Name:_____

     Address:_____   Address:_____

     _____   _____

     Tel No: _____   Tel No: _____

confidential franchise

questionnaire
Please complete in your own handwriting

PERSONAL DETAILS
(Joint applicants other than husband and wife should complete two separate forms.)

SURNAME:	
FORENAME(S):	
HOME ADDRESS:	
DAYTIME TEL NO:	
EVENING TEL NO:	
DATE OF BIRTH:	
MARITAL STATUS:	
HEALTH:	

FINANCIAL DETAILS

BANK:	
ADDRESS:	
HOW LONG ACCOUNT HELD:	
BUILDING SOCIETY:	
ADDRESS:	
BUSINESS INTERESTS:	
CAPITAL AVAILABLE FOR FRANCHISE:	

SUITABLITY
Please assess your ability to cope with the areas outlined below, marking from 1 (your weakest) to 6 (your strongest)

☐ DRIVE AND DETERMINATION

☐ PRACTICAL SKILLS

☐ SELF ORGANISATION

☐ MANAGEMENT OF MONEY

☐ SALES ABILITY

☐ MANAGEMENT OF PEOPLE

EMPLOYMENT HISTORY/PREVIOUS EXPERIENCE

CURRENT EMPLOYER
(or previous employer if less than 3 years with current employer)

NAME:	
ADDRESS:	
POSITION:	
TIME WITH THIS EMPLOYER	

PREVIOUS EMPLOYER
(if less than 3 years with current employer)

NAME:	
ADDRESS:	
POSITION:	
TIME WITH THIS EMPLOYER	

CURRENT BUSINESS *(if self employed)*

NAME:	
ADDRESS:	
TYPE OF BUSINESS:	
PREVIOUS BUSINESS EXPERIENCE:	

HAVE YOU, OR ANY BUSINESS IN WHICH YOU HAVE OWNED AN INTEREST, BEEN INVOLVED IN BANKRUPTCY, INSOLVENCY PROCEEDINGS OR COMPROMISE WITH CREDITORS?   ☐ YES   ☐ NO

IF YES PLEASE GIVE FULL DETAILS

SIGNATURE(S):

DATE:

Apollo Blinds
Cold Hesledon Ind. Estate
Seaham
Co. Durham, SR7 8ST

TEL: 0191 5130061
FAX: 0191 5130516
e-mail: franchising@apolloblinds.co.uk

20 January 2000

Dear John,

Franchising Opportunities with Apollo Blinds

It was a pleasure to speak to you today about franchising opportunities with Apollo blinds.

As you know, we are Britain's Biggest Blind Store Chain, with outlets throughout the U.K. and Ireland. However, I am pleased to say that your desired location is currently available.

We were most impressed with the quality of your application and our subsequent telephone coversation and would be delighted to take the discussion to the next level. Consequently, we have arranged for you to visit our headquarters in Seaham, County Durham on Tuesday February 1st 2000 at 11.00 a.m.

Please be kind enough to confirm the date and time with my personal assistant Sarah Jarvis, who will be only too pleased to provide you with travel details .

We look forward to meeting with you then,

Kind regards,

Graham Mylchreest
Director/General Manager.

APOLLO WINDOW BLINDS is a franchise owned and operated under licence
Reg. Office: Wellington House, New Zealand Avenue, Walton on Thames, Surrey KT12 1PY

without worrying about the effects on their loved ones. Finding out about their partner and children to see that any claimed support is genuine and strong is necessary.

Checking out finances, you must clearly be certain that the franchisee has enough money available to launch and sustain the venture. A blend of personal and loan finance may be advisable – wholly self-funded, and that driving edge could be lessened; totally borrowed and repayment commitments might be demoralising. Turning to their goals, you will wish to discover that they are achievable, given the restraints of franchising, otherwise you will find yourself with a discontented franchisee on your hands. Such objectives as becoming very rich, taking it easy and so on should flash warning signals to you.

An application form ought to give you enough positive or negative pointers to enable you to choose whether to meet the applicant or to reject them (which, if necessary, you should do promptly and politely in line with your normal recruitment procedure). A preliminary meeting may be arranged at the applicant's home where they will feel relaxed and able to answer your questions honestly. You will thus learn more from their replies, can assess their supportive loved ones (if appropriate) and gain a fuller picture of them. As a simple but effective example, a couple who live in a grubby and messy environment may allow their franchised outlet to deteriorate into the same condition.

Pose these queries to see how suited they are to franchising and your particular franchise.

- Tell me about yourself.
- What do your partner and dependents feel about franchising?
- How will it affect them?
- In what ways will they help you?
- Tell me about your education and qualifications.
- Why did you select those subjects?
- Have you ever had any health problems – what were they?
- How did they affect your work?
- Tell me about your free time activities.

- Describe your past and present work experiences.
- What do you do in an average day?
- What are your responsibilities?
- Do you work in a team or on your own?
- Which do you prefer?
- What do you like and dislike about your job?
- What do you find easy and difficult to do?

Moving on, you could also ask these questions:

- Tell me about your finances.
- What qualities do you think our franchisees should have?
- Why do you wish to become a franchisee?
- What attracts you to this franchise?
- What are your strengths and weaknesses, in relation to franchising?
- Where do you want to be in five, ten and fifteen years' time?
- May I see your driving licence, certificates, diplomas?
- Could I have permission to approach your two referees?

Naturally, the franchisee will wish to know more about your franchise package and will have many questions to put to you – see Meeting Franchisors, page 106. In addition to answering these at your first interview, you ought to set up a second meeting at your head office so that they can look around, talk to your team and piece together a better impression of you. If you have checked them out prior to this – investigating their credit rating, taking up references and so forth as you would usually do when entering into a business transaction or recruiting staff – you should be able to conclude their visit with a firm offer. If it is accepted, you can press on with the legalities of issuing the franchise (see Signing the Franchise Agreement, page 119).

Key Facts

The franchisor must commission a franchise consultant – who should be an affiliate of the BFA – to conduct a feasibility study of the franchisor's suitability for franchising. He or she then ought to work alongside the franchisor in developing and maintaining a winning franchise network.

Pilot schemes have to be set up and run to test and refine the format and to assess and blend together the correct mix of opening and continuing services to be provided for franchisees. An operating manual, a franchise agreement and a franchise prospectus ought to be drafted as well.

The franchisor should apply to become an associate member of the British Franchise Association which offers many advantages, not least that it will be a huge draw to those looking to purchase a franchise from a reputable and trustworthy franchisor.

The franchise package may be promoted through newspapers, magazines and directories and franchise exhibitions. Prospectuses and application forms should be given to interested potential franchisees. Successful applicants must then be interviewed at their home and the franchisor's head office and questioned about their personality, background, finances and goals. An offer should only be made after careful thought and analysis.

PART TWO: BECOMING A FRANCHISEE

5

FRANCHISING: THE ADVANTAGES AND DISADVANTAGES

If you're thinking of buying a franchise – or are a potential franchisor wishing to see a would-be franchisee's viewpoint – you must initially contemplate the advantages and disadvantages of franchising for a franchisee. Before spending further time and money pursuing your ambitions, you need to be absolutely convinced that the pros outweigh the cons and that this is what you really want to do.

The Advantages of Franchising

The main advantages of purchasing a respected franchise system – rather than setting up and running a small business on your own – are as follows. It offers:

- **a proven track record**
- **initial help and advice**
- **an established name**
- **continual support and guidance.**

A Proven Track Record

Prior to offering a franchise, the ethical franchisor will have administered a pilot scheme (or schemes) in suitable commercial circumstances for at least a year. There may now be other franchisees trading too. As a franchisee operating the same business along identical lines in similar conditions, your chances of success must be high (and certainly far greater than the lone business person beginning from scratch and slowly progressing on a trial and error basis). After all, a franchise system that has done well in Swansea, Ipswich and Glasgow ought to be equally profitable in Brighton, Nottingham and Newcastle.

Having a sound track record is especially advantageous when you are launching your franchised outlet, ensuring that you are viewed more favourably by business contacts than a wholly independent trader would be. As an example, most landlords are reluctant to rent their properties to small enterprises who may be here today, gone tomorrow, preferring trouble-free, long-term, large companies as their tenants (and those who do lease premises to one-off ventures almost inevitably set onerous terms, demanding substantial deposits and rent advances). With a highly successful franchise network behind you, many landlords will see you as part of a national chain and positively welcome you as an occupant.

Similarly, some high street banks, despite the image conveyed by television advertisements and promotional brochures, remain wary of backing new small businesses unless the owner is able to provide an equal, pound-for-pound investment and (often excessive) security for even the most modest loan or overdraft facility. With a proven franchise system, raising finance is usually easier. All of the leading banks now offer special financial packages for prospective franchisors on more favourable terms and conditions than those given to the totally independent trader. Of most help, a bank will require less capital (perhaps a third rather than a half of the total sum needed to start the venture) and security from you.

Initial Help and Advice

The reputable franchisor will actively assist a franchisee to set up a concern in every conceivable way – from assessing and selecting an operating territory and site through supplying equipment, machinery and stock, to training staff. All of the accumulated know-how from the pilot (and any other franchised) operations – even so far as the most appropriate colour, size and position of employees' lapel badges – should be made available.

This wholly comprehensive, hands-on service makes it less time-consuming and expensive for you to open a franchised outlet than the equivalent completely independent concern. The supportive franchisor already knows what and what not to do, having seen and done it all before several times. A new small trader has so much to discover – perhaps negotiating with a likely landlord, dealing with suppliers and managing staff for the first time – that it is normally a slow and occasionally painful learning process with some costly mistakes being made.

Such invaluable assistance may also enable you to begin trading as a franchisee with little or even no knowledge or experience of the particular business, trade or industry. The franchisor is always accessible, ready and willing to pass on the necessary information. To launch a venture alone without being able to draw upon some relevant background data would almost certainly lead to eventual failure. There would just be too much to find out about and too many potential pitfalls.

An Established Name

The solid and reputable franchisor who has established and then maintained a winning network will have gradually developed a well-known and universally respected reputation. Thus, you will automatically acquire a recognisable name, image and built-in goodwill. Within your territorial area you will have a standing – which you do not yet personally deserve – that would invariably take many months or more probably years to earn if you operated on your own.

Instantly possessing a memorable name and sound business status means that your sales and profits should increase at a faster and more substantial rate than those of the similar, new small enterprise. With renowned franchises such as *Home Tune*, *Prontaprint* and *Pizza*

Express, customers know exactly what to expect having seen, heard of or purchased from them before. If they want the particular products or services offered, they will buy without hesitation. Faced with the unknown *Chaplin's Car Tuning*, *The Printing Shop* and *Tony's Pizza Parlour*, possible customers are uncertain what they will receive. Most will wait to learn of their friends' and colleagues' experiences before parting with any money.

Continual Support and Guidance

With an ethical franchise, the franchisor is ever willing and able to help a franchisee as and when necessary, not only providing an operating manual that specifies all of the ingredients of a successful venture but also having troubleshooting experts on call to answer queries and resolve problems. The franchisee should further have full access to the franchisor's ongoing research and development facilities, should be able to participate in updating training programmes and make the most of bulk buying, regional and national advertising campaigns.

Having such extensive back-up support allows you to concentrate on administering your business on a daily basis, without the incessant pressure of needing to devise policies, systems and procedures as you go along. The fully independent trader is constantly having to make innovative, far-reaching decisions, selecting alternative courses of action, worrying whether the right choices have been made and often suffering the consequences when they were wrong. Also, your operating costs ought to be lower than those of the lone business person who cannot benefit from group research and development, buying and advertising arrangements.

The Disadvantages of Franchising

Most franchise systems have numerous inherent disadvantages which you ought to be aware of. A franchise usually means:

- **hard work and effort**
- **constant payments**
- **inflexible rules and procedures**
- **mutual dependence.**

Hard Work and Effort

Franchising is far from the easy get-rich-quick scheme that many naive would-be franchisees believe it to be. Setting up any concern – searching and negotiating for a suitable property, applying for planning permission, raising funds, fitting out and stocking premises – requires hard work and effort, and there are limited financial rewards until the business is well established. Nor does the franchisor do everything for the franchisee as some fondly imagine they do. You will be fully involved in launching the business and wholly responsible for its day-to-day running thereafter – ordering and displaying stock, dealing with demanding customers, handling awkward staff, doing the accounts and so on.

If the venture is to succeed – and it is ultimately up to you to maximise the potential of the franchise system – you must be prepared to work long and often unsociable hours. A twelve-hour day, seven-day week is usual. You'll probably have to tidy round, check on supplies and tackle the post before trading begins, be on call through tea and lunch breaks until it ends and tot up the takings, do the books and collect replacement stock in the evenings and weekends. Days off and holidays will be minimal or non-existent, especially in the first few years. Even when you're not working, you'll find yourself continually thinking about the business. It is difficult – if not impossible – to switch off and relax.

Financial sacrifices may have to be made as well. Initial profits will grow slowly, usually taking three years or more to provide a full return on your investment (and be extremely wary of any franchisor who promises instant riches). To finance the concern, you could have to arrange a substantial loan, overdraft or second mortgage which needs to be repaid from your slender profits. Thus, you'll possibly be unable to afford to pay for any luxuries in the foreseeable future, which can be distressing, especially if you have children who perhaps have to miss longed-for school trips and holidays.

Constant Payments

After handing over an initial fee to cover the costs of setting up, the franchisee usually then has to make regular royalty payments to the franchisor in exchange for continuing back-up support. Normally based on turnover net of VAT (from as little as 2.5 per cent to as much as 30 per cent plus), often subject to a minimum amount (so that the franchisor is guaranteed a certain income even during difficult trading conditions) and paid out every week, month or quarter (depending on the franchise), these payments can create immense friction between the franchisor and franchisee.

Typically, the franchisor may pressurise you to try to improve takings, regardless of your current excessive workload and efforts. You could even be forced – under the terms of the franchise – to participate in commercial activities such as advertising and promotional campaigns which increase sales but not profits (because any profits generated by such actions are cancelled out by the extra costs incurred). Minimum payments might cause severe financial problems for you if sales plummet during a seasonal lull or a recession. Also, as you become more experienced and the franchisor's help and advice is naturally less visible, you may begin to resent paying out so much for so long when you appear to be receiving so little in return.

Inflexible Rules and Procedures

The franchisee has to operate according to strict guidelines covering every aspect of the business. Fully detailed within the franchisor's operating manual, these ensure that high, uniform standards are maintained so the success story continues for everyone. The franchisor will carry out regular checks to make certain that the carefully devised rules and procedures are being scrupulously followed at all times, and as a last resort can terminate the agreement and remove the franchisee from the network if they are not.

Having to operate an identikit venture under the ever watchful eye of the franchisor can be extremely irritating even though such close control is understandable. Sometimes, you will feel that you are little more than a glorified manager with all of the responsibility but none of the power to make any significant decisions.

Franchising is unlikely to be a suitable form of self-employment if you are staunchly independent or entrepreneurial by nature; it could be far too frustrating for you to work in this way, and your relationship with the franchisor would inevitably break down, irreparably damaging your concern.

Occasionally, you may even believe such restrictions are harming your own particular operation. You could perhaps feel that the decor is dated, suppliers' standards are falling or products or services need to be amended or replaced to cater for the changing needs of your local customers. Any alterations will be difficult to implement unless you are able to secure agreement from the franchisor and the other franchisees that you will all introduce changes together (and if you go ahead on your own you risk losing your franchise).

Should you wish to sell your business as a going concern, the franchisor can vet and – if appropriate – reject your potential buyer as an unsuitable franchisee. It could take months or years for you to find an acceptable purchaser who will be allowed to take over your concern and join the franchisor's network.

Mutual Dependence

The franchisor and all of the franchisees are totally dependent on each other for their continued success. The franchisor provides the established format, respected name, detailed operating manual, constant help and guidance, and so on. The franchisees pay an initial fee, follow the agreed rules and procedures, maintain (and hopefully develop) the good reputation of the franchise system, pay royalties on time, and so forth. Clearly, you could suffer from such an all for one, one for all approach if the franchisor or other franchisees do not fulfil their respective obligations.

The franchisor may be unable or unwilling to supply satisfactory support and advice, could make mistakes when researching and developing new ideas for the system or might even become insolvent, leaving you to struggle on in isolation. Other franchisees may break away from the set format, perhaps selling cheaper, substandard products or offering lower standards of service than are expected. They could be featured in the media for mistreating their staff, upsetting their customers or breaking the law. Like it or not, this will reflect on you and damage your business – perhaps fatally.

Key Facts

There are many important advantages of franchising for the franchisee. A tried and tested system is purchased. Expert help and guidance are provided to launch the franchised venture. A well-known trading name and reputation are immediately attached to the franchisee. Ongoing support is always available. These then create other plus points for the franchisee.

There are several relevant disadvantages of franchising for the franchisee. He or she must work long and hard to succeed. Regular payments have to be made to the franchisor for the back-up services. Franchising is a rigid and inflexible trading method. The franchisee and franchisor are wholly reliant on each other. These then produce more minus points for the franchise.

6

EVALUATING YOURSELF

Believing that franchising is worth further investigation, you must fully appraise your personality, background, finances and goals to see whether or not you are likely to be suitable. All winning franchisees share certain similarities which you ought to be able to recognise within yourself if you are to succeed. Should they not exist, it would be wise to withdraw your interest now rather than later when you will have invested so much more time and money, only to fail because you are wholly unsuited to this form of self-employment.

Appraising Your Personality

Even though the franchisor makes all of the major decisions and the operating manual provides a detailed and rigid framework in which to work, you do have to be independent enough to take day-to-day decisions on your own – such as the amount and timing of stock deliveries, hiring and firing of staff, and so on. Should these be unduly delayed or not made at all, your business could suffer accordingly. For example, failing to swiftly rectify an employee's persistent below-par performance might irreparably affect customer relations and team morale. Also, constantly looking for a second opinion or approval will eventually create ill feeling between you and the franchisor, who will resent having to do everything for you.

At the same time, you need to be sufficiently self-disciplined to accept the franchisor's close and continued control of your venture, being willing to listen and act on suggestions and (hopefully constructive) criticisms without bias or resentment. If you cannot – and are always seeking to exert your individuality, perhaps by changing layout and decor, raising or lowering prices, and so forth – then your working relationship with the franchisor will rapidly deteriorate to the stage where you risk expulsion from the network.

You ought to be a self-starter too, ambitious enough to want to make a success of this and – in time – other franchised ventures, and suitably determined to work incessantly to ensure that your dreams turn into reality. Should you simply wish to plod along earning a modest living from a 9-to-5, five-days per week job, you are unlikely to cope well with the immense workload and ever present financial pressures that exist in the early days of the enterprise. Nor will you withstand the ongoing demands of the franchisor, steadily pressurising you to keep improving your takings (thus raising the royalties due to be handed over).

Getting on well with people – the (demanding) franchisor, (lively) staff and (awkward) customers – is another quality which you really have to possess. A distant or strained relationship with the franchisor may mean that much needed back-up support – training, updating and so on – is not as forthcoming as it might be. Poorly treated, discontented employees could take out their dissatisfaction on your customer. A reluctance to deal cheerfully with the public may persuade them to take their business elsewhere.

You need to be honest so that the all-important franchisor/ franchisee partnership can develop into a mutually comfortable and satisfying relationship, with give and take on both sides. If the franchisor trusts you – to follow the format implicitly, work hard, maximise sales, fully declare turnover, pay royalties on time and so forth – then much of that suffocating close control and many of those embarrassing check-ups will be reduced, leaving you to operate the concern without unwanted supervision. Should doubts and suspicion exist, they could increase to unpleasant levels.

Thinking About Your Background

Having an in-depth knowledge of the territory in which you will trade can be extremely useful, as existing business and would-be customer contacts may help you to establish your venture far quicker than an unfamiliar franchisee could hope to do. Some organisational, administrative and financial skills and experience would be beneficial too, enabling you to understand the outlet swiftly and then run it efficiently in accordance with the franchisor's rules and regulations.

Perhaps surprisingly, a total lack of previous experience of the same work, trade or industry is often most desirable as it makes it much easier for the franchisor to train you to use the systems and procedures of the particular business format. The owners and managers of *Chaplin's Car Tuning*, *The Printing Shop* and *Tony's Pizza Parlour* would probably not be welcomed by the franchisors of comparable ventures because they could be too set in their ways. It is difficult to completely eliminate and then wholly replace ingrained ideas and work patterns. Few franchisors want to attempt it.

You must be in good mental and physical health to be a winner in the franchise market. Mentally, you have to be tough enough to handle the initial loss of job security, the mix of low income, high expenditure and escalating debts, plus a significant drop in living standards. Physically, you need to be sufficiently strong to labour on well into the evenings and at weekends, often performing strenuous tasks such as lifting, carrying and cleaning if you cannot afford to employ staff to do them for you. It is hard to take time off as the franchisor and any employees are unlikely to be both willing and able to run your business for you.

Family support is equally essential so that you can concentrate on making a success of the venture without feeling guilty or having to worry about its effects on your partner and children. Starting any concern takes up all the owner's available time, energy and money and his or her family need to be aware of and completely accept the consequences – which can vary from rearranged mealtimes through missed treats to helping out as and when required. If they cannot come to terms with the inevitable changes in their lifestyle then intolerable strain can be put on business and personal relationships.

Considering Your Finances

Not surprisingly, you must have sufficient money available to commence and maintain your franchised concern, without expecting to recoup the investment for three years or so. You probably already know the type of franchise and work activity that are likely to be most suited to you and may also have a very approximate idea of the possible costs and returns involved. You now have to roughly calculate your financial resources and limits so that if or (hopefully) when you begin your search for the right franchise, you will know which opportunities you can and cannot afford to pursue further.

As a quick guide, add up all of your assets – house, inheritance or redundancy money, savings, stocks and shares, life assurance, pension schemes, car, antiques, jewellery, paintings and so on. Decide which you can and – more importantly, want – to invest in the venture. You may not be prepared to sell your home to move into a tiny flat above a franchised shop if you have a young and growing family. Similarly, you could be unwilling to use that inheritance which has so far funded your children's education. Then, deduct all of your liabilities – mortgage, loans, overdraft, tax payments, credit card bills and so forth – to see what remains for franchising. You may find it helpful to complete a financial audit analysis as shown opposite.

Have a provisional talk to a bank manager to discover whether or not additional finance might be obtainable, perhaps a loan to start the enterprise and an overdraft facility to keep it going until you are making substantial profits. As franchising with a reputable franchisor offers relatively safe and secure prospects, you may have to provide only 30 to 35 per cent of the total capital yourself (instead of the usual 50 per cent for small business people), with the balance forwarded by the bank. Security requirements could be less stringent too, especially if the franchisor supplies extensive and verifiable financial data for you. For further information, contact the franchise units of the major high street banks (see Appendix D, page 164).

***** **CONFIDENTIAL INFORMATION** *****

Please complete this page and bring it with you to your initial interview

PERSONAL FINANCIAL AUDIT

ASSETS

Value of home	£
Value of vehicles	£
Value of shares and trusts	£
Other savings such as building societies	£
Cash in bank	£
Any other assets _____ _____	£
TOTAL ASSETS	£

LIABILITIES

1	O/s mortgage	£
2	O/s hire purchase	£
3	O/s credit cards O/s gas/electricity/rates	£
4	Any other liabilities _____ _____	£
	TOTAL LIABILITIES	£

MONTHLY OUTGOINGS

Mortgage repayments	£
Insurance premiums	£
Fuel (gas, electricity etc)	£
Rates	£
Hire purchase	£
Pensions and life assurances	£
Food, clothing and entertainment	£
School fees	£
Other outgoings _____ _____	£
TOTAL OUTGOINGS	£

PLEASE NOTE ALSO ANY OTHER FINANCIAL MATTERS THAT COULD BE OF IMPORTANCE

Contemplating Your Goals

Finishing off your frank and realistic self-appraisal, you must think about why you want to go into franchising and what you wish to achieve from it. Write out all of the reasons for your interest: to break away from a 9-to-5 routine, to be your own boss, to do something with your life after being made redundant rather than drifting into retirement, and so on. Then jot down your personal and business goals: to take life a little easier, to spend more time with your family, to open a string of ventures, to make your fortune, and so forth. Be brutally honest with yourself, always listing your private, off-the-record causes and targets, however trivial or outrageous they may appear to be.

One by one, study each of them in comparison with the advantages and disadvantages of franchising to see how well matched they are to this particular trading method. Remaining in your existing employment or starting up a wholly independent concern could be better in the circumstances. For example, franchising will enable you to escape from that 9-to-5 monotony but not to take things easy, as you will have to toil twice as hard and long to make a decent living. Similarly, it will allow you to work for yourself although the only way to be with your loved ones will be to bring them into the business alongside you.

Regardless of your reasons and goals – which will obviously differ considerably from one person to another – you do have to be certain within yourself that they tally with the particular mix of pros and cons that are commonly associated with franchising. If any of your targets are likely to be difficult or even impossible to reach (making a fortune as a franchisee is an unrealistic pipe-dream) then you would be extremely wise to terminate your plans at this stage, because only frustration, disappointment and unhappiness lie ahead for you.

Key Facts

The successful franchisee must be both independent and disciplined. Being a self-starter is necessary too. He or she should be able to mix with people. Honesty is also an important quality.

Possessing a hands-on knowledge of the prospective territory may be beneficial. A lack of similar work experience could be advantageous. Good mental and physical health is essential. Family support is vital as well.

The winning franchisee must have sufficient funds to start and run his or her franchised concern, expecting to recoup the capital investment only after several years.

The personal and business goals of the franchisee ought to be suited to franchising and its individual blend of advantages and disadvantages.

7

SELECTING A FRANCHISE

If you are totally convinced that you possess all of the key characteristics needed to be successful, you must move on to begin your search for a winning franchise. You should draw up a shortlist of opportunities, obtain prospectuses, meet the franchisors and take further advice before making your choice of the most suitable franchise in your circumstances. Always investigate in a careful and systematic manner, and don't be reluctant to withdraw at any stage if you find out that a particular franchise – or even franchising itself – is wrong for you.

Shortlisting Franchise Opportunities

To shortlist properly, you need to start with as full a list of franchises as possible. Otherwise, the one that you missed, and which you discover six months later when you've signed up with someone else, inevitably turns out to be the most appropriate in your situation. You can compile a hopefully complete list, along with thumbnail sketches of each, by checking with a variety of sources, most of which will also give you helpful general information about the do's and don'ts of franchising.

The British Franchise Association can supply a Franchising Information Pack with up-to-date listings of its members and the same list, constantly up-dated, appears on their web site at www.british-franchise.org.uk. Having to undergo strict accreditation processes and subject to stringent codes of business practice to join and remain within this internationally respected trade organisation, these franchisors arguably provide the safest and most reputable franchises in the market place. Although your subsequent commercial success cannot be guaranteed, they are certainly worth very serious consideration indeed. In addition to these important listings, the pack contains newsletters, handy booklets and information sheets giving practical down-to-earth advice on evaluating franchises plus details of established professional bodies – such as banks, solicitors and accountants – which are afiliated to the BFA. For further information, see Appendix B (page 152), Appendix C (page 159) and Appendix D (page 164). Read 'Joining the BFA' (page 51) too.

National and regional newspapers and business orientated magazines should be studied as they are published, perhaps in your local library or friendly newsagent. Many regularly carry franchise features and advertisements from which you can further develop your list and – of equal significance – your understanding of franchising. In particular, the Daily Express looks at the franchise market in its 'Business Plus' section every Monday. The Times, Daily Telegraph, Daily Mail, and their sister Sunday newspapers, often focus in on franchising as well.

Specialist trade magazines, including Business Franchise Magazine, Franchise World, The Franchise Magazine and Franchise, ought to be purchased on publication or subscribed to. They all incorporate lists of the latest franchise opportunities, both BFA and non-BFA members. Articles from leading experts in franchise management, banking, law and accountancy, news of past, present and future events plus advertisements from franchisors and other organisations associated with the trade will be of supplementary interest to you. For more details, refer to Appendix F, page 172.

Various directories – namely Franchise World Directory, The Business Franchise Directory and The United Kingdom Franchise Directory – are published every year and should be available for inspection in most larger libraries, or can be bought direct from the publishers. They probably set out the widest range of franchises currently on offer and in the greatest depth. Assorted features on different aspects of the franchising industry are essential reading too.

Again, see Appendix F, page 172. Franchise exhibitions – such as the Scottish Franchise Exhibition in Glasgow, the Spring National Franchise Exhibition in London and the Autumn National Franchise Exhibition in Birmingham – are always worth a prolonged visit. You can expand your list of franchises, pick up franchisors' literature and attend the daily seminars run by specialists in their field. These exhibitions tend to be at the same venues at similar times each year – several are referred to in Appendix E, page 171. Additional information can be supplied by the various national franchise associations listed in Appendix A, page 149.

Miscellaneous other sources may help you to complete your list. Your bank manager, solicitor, accountant, work colleagues, friends and relatives could have heard of or read about a franchise that you had overlooked and which might be right for you. Tell everyone and anyone you know that you're interested in franchising. Let them be extra ears and eyes for you. Check out Appendix G, page 174.

Taking your long list, you must then read through the brief notes that you will have accumulated about each franchise – type, activities and so on – which should enable you to compile your shortlist of potentially ideal franchises. Typically, you will eliminate some opportunities because they are the wrong type for you. Perhaps you are seeking a job rather than a business or investment franchise. Others will be struck off as the work does not suit your individual personality or background. You may be unable to face the prospect of clearing out drains every day. Most of the remaining franchises will be deleted for financial reasons; inevitably, you will have limited funds available to launch and maintain a business. Hopefully, you will find yourself left with between three and six franchises to study and choose from.

Obtaining Franchise Prospectuses

Your initial contact with the shortlisted franchisors ought to be a simple request for a prospectus, which is a promotional brochure that will tell you more about the franchisor and the format, products and services, finances, contract and network, plus the type of franchisee required. An application form is usually included as well. Writing off for a prospectus is normally wiser than talking to the franchisor on the telephone or at any exhibition as a conversation can so easily develop into an interview which you are not yet ready for. Extracts from examples of franchise prospectuses are reproduced on pages 45 and 51, with thanks to Apollo and Travail.

On receiving the prospectuses – which will vary enormously in length and details from one franchisor to another – you need to consider exactly what you want to know about the franchisor, format, products and services and so forth. You may find it helpful to jot down the key criteria that you're looking for beneath those loose and informal headings. Obviously, a brochure cannot supply all the information required, but should give you enough positive or negative pointers for you to decide whether or not you wish to submit an application.

Regarding the *franchisor*, you must study the prospectus for signs of sufficient experience of business, franchising and the industry to have faced every conceivable opportunity and challenge, thus maximising your chances of being comprehensively taught and assisted. Having a lengthy track record, links with a multi-resourced major company and executives with appropriate skills, knowledge and backgrounds may be plus points. Evidence of ethical behaviour is very necessary so that you can trust and rely on any help and advice given. Belonging to the BFA and producing a clear and detailed, froth-free brochure with data about bankers, accountants and so on are favourable indicators.

Compatible goals are equally important, offering reassurance that you will both be moving in the same direction. For example, a franchisor's oft-stated wish that they will be constantly introducing innovative goods may be worrying, as this could raise your costs and the risk of failure. Financial stability is absolutely essential if initial and ongoing services are to be promptly and efficiently provided at all times. Being part of a large and secure company might again be in the franchisor's favour.

Concerning the *business format*, you want to see that it has been fully tried and tested, therefore increasing the likelihood that you are buying a problem-free, winning formula. Having run a number of pilot operations in different localities for over a year is a plus (with established franchisees making it an even better prospect). It should also have one or more distinctive features which set it apart so that customers will come to you instead of to competitors. The trading name, a memorable slogan, even product packaging could be picked out as the special ingredients that you're seeking.

The format further needs to be be comprehensive so that you can start and administer your venture with little or no experience, yet simple enough for you to quickly master all aspects of it. Services such as finding the right site, helping to obtain funds, supplying stock and other supplies, pre- and post-opening advertising, assisting with insurance, initial and ongoing training, sending along a launch team, handing over an operating manual simplifying systems and procedures, carrying out continual research and development and having trouble-shooting experts on call, will hopefully be incorporated within it and thus mentioned in the brochure.

Checking out the **products and services**, you should look for indications that they will sell steadily every week, month and year, in order that you can invest in the franchised concern with confidence. Offering a long-established and varied range of goods, each with a number of unique selling points and patent, trade mark and design protection (as appropriate) to prevent competitors directly copying them, are all good signs. So too is trading in a large and growing market that is unaffected by seasonal or fashion trends. You must then look for proof that your products and services will sell at premium prices, so you can achieve a satisfactory return for your expenditure (bearing in mind that the franchisor will probably be taking a share of your takings via royalty payments). Selling goods with high mark-ups and profit margins in a price insensitive, usually exclusive market is desirable.

Referring to **finances**, you ought to be sure that the franchise package represents value for money. Should you subsequently discover that you are paying over the odds, your relationship with the franchisor will become completely untenable. A profit-free initial fee which simply covers the costs of putting together the franchise, setting-up expenses that are roughly identical with those of a wholly independent trader, and on-going fees from only one source – either a percentage of your turnover net of VAT or a mark-up or commission on supplies – are all positive features. Royalty fees that are not subject to a minimum level, are paid monthly or quarterly rather than weekly in arrears and which reduce as you become more experienced and self-sufficient are most fair to you.

Similarly, you need to be certain that the package will generate sufficient turnover and profit to make a reasonable living for you and your family. Projected figures which are in line with those of comparable businesses, that are based on franchisees' actual trading accounts and which indicate a return on your investment in no less than three years are most believable.

With regard to the *franchise contract*, you should be scanning the prospectus for firm suggestions that it is fair and reasonable, thus ensuring that you can establish and sustain a mutually satisfying relationship with the franchisor. The key points to watch out for include a 5-year plus contract that allows you time to recoup your money and make an acceptable profit, clearly detailed rights and responsibilities, an independent arbitration arrangement to settle disagreements, perhaps through the BFA, and the freedom to sell the franchise whenever you wish either to the franchisor at its true market value or to another party subject to the franchisor's permission which shall not be unreasonably withheld. The franchisor should not make any money out of the transfer.

Also check that you can terminate the franchise without a financial penalty if you are unhappy, ill or making inadequate profits, that you will be given every chance to rectify contractual breaches and will be compensated for your goodwill, stock and equipment in the event of termination by the franchisor. On expiry, you ought to be entitled to renew the franchise for the same period on similar terms without any significant additional fees. If the franchise is not renewed, you must be allowed to sell your stock and equipment on the open market or to the franchisor at realistic market prices.

Thinking of the *network*, you want to know that it is successful, which makes it increasingly likely that you will be too. A growing number of franchisees, some renewing their franchise and others taking on a second or third one, are positive indicators. A communicative network is significant as well so that constructive criticisms and suggestions may be exchanged and a healthy, amicable relationship can be maintained. Look for references to newsletters, regular franchisor/franchisee get togethers and franchise advisory committees (which represent all the franchisees in the network).

Try to calculate how important franchising is to the franchisor. The greater the income in comparison to self-owned units, the more committed and enthusiastic they will tend to be. See how many franchisor and franchisee owned operations exist. A slow and steady expansion of the network is far better than a fast and rapidly developing one which could leave the franchisor over-stretched and unable to perform services properly. Check the past, present and future growth rates of franchisor and franchisee owned outlets.

Reading about the *type of franchisee wanted*, you will hope to find that the qualities listed – such as territorial knowledge, robust health and so on – tally with those which you recognised from your vigorous self-appraisal. If they do – and all of the other (albeit incomplete) signs appear to be positive – you can then fully and honestly fill out the application form and return it to the franchisor. Two typical forms seeking initial information, are reproduced on pages 80 and 84.

Meeting Franchisors

If an application is favourably received, you will then be invited to meet the franchisor so that you can get to know each other and decide whether or not you are well matched and able to work together for mutual commercial benefits. Although every franchisor will adopt a slightly different recruitment procedure (refer to Recruiting Franchisees, page 71), you may perhaps have an initial interview in the familiar surroundings of your home. Following this, you could possibly be asked to go to the franchisor's head office to talk to the team. Seeing the other party in their own environment often enables you to form the most comprehensive and accurate impression of them.

Whatever the venue, you will want to check carefully and then build upon the basic (and generally favourable) information that you have already obtained from the various listings and the prospectus, posing questions and asking to see substantiating documents concerning the franchisor, format, products and services and so on. At the same time, the franchisor will press you about your personality, background, finances and goals, picking up and expanding upon the statements and any verifying material given in or attached to your application form.

Ever mindful of the key criteria that you wish to see, you may raise some (or even all) of the following queries about the franchisor, noting the answers and taking away any documents provided for subsequent discussion with and analysis by professional advisers such as accountants and solicitors.

- How long have you been trading?
- When did you begin franchising?
- How is your business structured?
- Who are your executives?
- What are their career histories?
- Are you a BFA member – if not, why not?
- What are your objectives?
- May I meet all of your team?
- Could you supply three years' audited accounts, your latest trading figures and commercial references?

Moving on to the business format, you could ask:

- Is this a new or proven format?
- How many pilot schemes have you set up and run?
- How long and where have these been operated?
- What is so special about the format?
- How will you help me to choose a territory and commercial property?
- What selection criteria will be used?

- How will you assist me to raise the finance?
- If you have made financial arrangements with a bank, what are the details?
- Who will provide my stock, equipment and machinery, and under what terms and conditions?
- What pre-launch advertising and promotion will be carried out?
- How will you help me to fully insure myself?
- Should you have made insurance arrangements with an insurance company, what are the details?
- What, where and when will you teach me to administer the concern?
- Will you give me on-site assistance when I begin trading – if so, who and for how long?

Also ask these questions:

- What business systems are supplied by you?
- What procedures must be followed?
- How and when do you check that these systems and procedures are being adhered to?
- How long will I have to rectify faults?
- How will you help me to make amends?
- What ongoing research and development is carried out?
- Where are new ideas tested?
- How often is the operating manual updated?
- When was it last rewritten?
- What, where and when will retraining take place?
- What trouble-shooting services will you provide for me?
- What, where and how often will advertising and promotion campaigns be conducted?
- May I see pilot accounts, a map and a market survey of my earmarked territory, plus a copy of the lease on the proposed premises, if appropriate?
- Could I have relevant bank and insurance company literature, stock and equipment brochures, examples of advertising and promotional material, your training programme and the operating

manual? (which you should be allowed to look at but not take away since it contains highly confidential data).

When talking about the products and services, you might put these queries to the franchisor:

- What products and services will I be offering?
- How long have they been on the market?
- What are their strengths and weaknesses?
- Are they protected in any way?
- What are their buying and selling prices?
- How would you describe the market?
- Who, how many and where are the customers?
- Why, when and how often do they buy the products and services?
- Who, how many and where are the competitors?
- How do they compare with what we have to offer?
- What is your market share?
- How will this be maintained or increased?
- May I see all of the products that I shall be selling?
- Could I watch the services being performed?
- May I have copies of any market research surveys?

Turning to finance, you ought to obtain answers to these particular questions:

- How much is the initial fee?
- When must this be handed over?
- What exactly am I paying for?
- What other start-up costs will be incurred by me?
- How much are the royalty fees?
- When must these be paid?
- What do I receive for my money?
- Do you mark up stock, equipment and machinery provided by you – if so, by how much?
- Are you on commission for products and services purchased by me from recommended suppliers? – if yes, how much?

- Is there a separate advertising levy – if so, how much and when must it be paid?
- How else will you make money from me?
- What are your sales, direct costs, overheads and profit projections for the first three to five years of my venture?
- How much working capital will be required?
- When will I derive a full return on my investment?
- How did you arrive at these figures?
- May I have detailed monthly profit and cash flow forecasts for the next three to five years?

Proceeding on to the contract, it is sensible to bring these queries to the franchisor's attention:

- How long is the franchise for?
- What are our respective rights and responsibilities to each other?
- How will disputes be amicably resolved?
- Are there arbitration arrangements?
- What are the rules and procedures for assigning the franchise?
- How may either party terminate the franchise prior to its expiry?
- What if I am taken permanently ill or die?
- What if either side becomes insolvent?
- What happens on expiry of the franchise?
- What are the terms and conditions for renewing the franchise?
- What happens to the goodwill, stock, equipment and machinery if the franchise is terminated or not renewed?
- May I have a copy of the franchise agreement?

Whilst discussing the franchise network, draw these questions into the conversation:

- How many company owned and franchised outlets do you have?
- Where and when were they opened?
- How many franchisees have renewed their franchise with you?
- Have any of your franchisees bought two or more franchises from you?

- How many franchisees have ceased trading or sold their franchise to a new franchisee or back to you?
- What were their reasons?
- Have you ever sued any of your franchisees or expelled them from the network?
- Why did you do this?
- How do you keep in touch with each other?
- How much of your income is derived from franchising?
- How many more company owned and franchised operations will you set up?
- When and whereabouts will they start trading?
- May I see a complete list of your franchisees' names and addresses and have permission to contact any of them?
- Could I also have a random selection of your franchisees' accounts?

Of course, the franchisor will want to question you to confirm that your personality, background, finances and goals are really suited to franchising and his or her individual system. Having already conducted your self-assessment, read about the type of person required and completed an application form, you should be able to answer each and every query to the franchisor's satisfaction. Hopefully, an offer to join the network will then be made to you (see Recruiting Franchisees, page 71).

Taking Further Advice

Having previously obtained some background information and advice when compiling your shortlist, and with all the evidence from the prospectus and meetings appearing to be highly favourable, it is tempting to commit yourself immediately to the franchise by signing a legally binding agreement. With your lifestyle, finances and future happiness at stake, it is wiser to conduct further investigations, talking to other franchisees and discussing your accumulated notes, thoughts and any substantiating material with professional experts before making your choice. Thus, you are far more likely to reach the correct decision in your circumstances.

With permission from the franchisor, approach as many of the franchisees as possible, tactfully side-stepping his or her potentially biased recommendations and choosing those with ventures in areas that are similar to your own proposed territory. Spending a minimum of two days with each of at least three franchisees should enable you to gain a fuller and more accurate, hands-on impression of the whole package and the ways in which it operates day-to-day. This may help you to calculate whether or not it is right for you.

Also, you can chat informally to the franchisees, repeating many of the same questions that you put to the franchisor and gaining an invaluable second opinion of the various topics but from the opposing viewpoint. These additional queries could also produce revealing replies.

- Has the franchisor always acted in an ethical manner – if not, what happened?
- Have initial and ongoing services been prompt, efficient and effective at all times – if not, why was this?
- How successful have the format, systems and procedures proved to be?
- What problems have you experienced with them – and how were they rectified?
- Is the operating manual comprehensive and clear – if not, what are its precise faults?
- How well do the goods sell?
- What are the profit margins?
- How many returns do you receive each month?
- How accurate were the financial projections – what errors were made and why?
- When did you obtain a complete return on your investment?
- Has the franchise represented value for money?
- Is the contract fair and balanced – if not, what changes would you make to it?
- How do you get along with the franchisor and other franchisees?

- Have you ever had any disagreements – if yes, what and how were they resolved?
- Will you renew your franchise?
- Would you do it all over again? If yes – why? If no – why not?

Now start seeking professional advice; the winning franchisee is one who is aware of his or her limitations and turns to others for assistance at this stage instead of going on alone. Take up the franchisor's commercial references – from banks, suppliers and so forth – hopefully confirming that they are experienced, ethical and have compatible goals and financial stability. If the franchisor is a company, look at their annual accounts at Companies House as they have a statutory obligation to register them there every year. Although you may already have these, the examination could throw up other helpful, undisclosed data – their formal objectives, executives' shares and so on. Contact credit reference agencies to see if their records reveal adverse details about the franchisor and/or executives, such as county court judgements for bad debts (see Appendix G, page 174, for addresses and telephone numbers).

Any new financial facts uncovered about the franchisor – with the three years' audited accounts, latest trading figures, pilot and franchisees' accounts plus profit and cash flow forecasts given to you earlier – must be studied and appraised by an accountant (and a bank manager if you are borrowing funds) rather than you. Too many naive would-be franchisees buy a book on accounting techniques and methods, read it and think they know enough to correctly interpret the complex and carefully composed figures submitted to them. It is these people who are most at risk of being exploited by unscrupulous franchisors (although they have no one to blame but themselves). Pick an accountant who has been recommended by a fellow-trader, is a member of the Chartered Association of Certified Accountants or the Institute of Chartered Accountants – and leave the detailed analysis to them. See Appendix G, page 174 for further information.

Your accountant will peruse the pilot accounts and tell you if the format seems to be financially proven, whilst you continue to investigate whether it is distinctive, comprehensive and simple. You will want to inspect the territory and any premises allocated to you, taking along a map, notes of their selection criteria (to see they are really met) and any market survey on their viability (to check that it is accurate). Discuss the various criteria with a local business transfer or estate agent who knows the area and property market well to discover how valid they are and if any other ones ought to have been thought of by the franchisor. Find an agent who belongs to the Institution of Business Agents, The Incorporated Society of Valuers and Auctioneers or the National Association of Estate Agents. Call in a surveyor who is a member of the Royal Institution of Chartered Surveyors to assess the premises. Have a solicitor – who *must* be well versed in the franchise world – to look over the lease and heed his or her comments. (Refer to Appendix D, page 164, and Appendix G, page 174)

Also, you will wish to study any bank and/or insurance schemes offered by the franchisor, to ascertain how they relate to alternative packages available. Talk to the managers of the remaining high street banks and an insurance broker belonging to The British Insurance and Investment Brokers Association. Appraise stock, equipment and machinery – quality, prices and so forth – alongside those sold on the open market. Your nearest Chamber of Commerce or Trade should be able to put you in touch with nearby suppliers. You could want further opinions about the franchisor's advertising, promotional and training programmes. Your regional enterprise agency – reached through the administering body, Business in the Community – or a small business association or the Small Firms Service may be worth contacting (and can give widespread advice on other small business topics too). Check Appendix G, page 174, for relevant data.

Looking at the products and services, you can go out and about to actually compare their range, prices, positive and negative features and so on with their competitors. Product protection organisations such as the Design Registry and the Patent Office will supply details about protecting them from being copied. To confirm the current size and anticipated growth rate of the local market, see if the findings of the franchisor's survey match the comments from your Chamber of Commerce or Trade. Further afield, various research organisations such as Jordans Business Information Service and Mintel

International – regularly publish reports analysing the performances of different business sectors, industries and markets. Once more, see Appendix G, page 174. With your accountant having stated that the finances are all sound, your appropriately experienced solicitor telling you that the contract is fair and reasonable, and the franchisees having confirmed that they belong to a successful network, you must now be able to decide if this franchise is the one for you. If it is, you should then accept the franchisor's offer and press ahead with the legal arrangements for taking up the franchise. Refer to 'Signing the Franchise Agreement', page 119.

Key Facts

A full list of available franchises must be compiled by the potential franchisee if he or she is to shortlist properly. This may be built up by contacting the BFA, reading newspapers, business magazines, franchise magazines and directories, visiting franchise exhibitions and telling all professional and personal associates about his or her interest. Those franchisors who sell franchises of the right type and which suit the would-be franchisee's tastes and finances can then be shortlist.

The prospective franchisee must ask for a prospectus from each franchisor, subsequently studying it for favourable information about the franchisor, format, products, service, finances, contract and network plus details of the type of person wanted. If appropriate, an application form should be completed and submitted to the franchisor.

Once a successful application has been processed, the potential franchisee will be invited to meet the franchisor. He or she must take this as an opportunity to check facts given in the prospectus, to develop a wider understanding of the particular package and to collect verifying material to be analysed in association with professional advisers.

Before accepting an offer from the franchisor, the would-be franchisee ought to spend time in various businesses within the network, chatting to franchisees about the package. He or she must also carry out further investigations, drawing on expert advice when necessary. The correct franchise should then be chosen.

PART THREE: GETTING TOGETHER

8

SIGNING THE FRANCHISE AGREEMENT

Whether you are a franchisor or soon to be franchisee, you should now have liaised with a solicitor who is fully familiar with franchising and be ready to tie yourself to the other party by signing a franchise contract. As this is the bedrock of your relationship – reluctantly referred to in times of trouble – it needs to be comprehensive, unambiguous and even-handed. Beneath the broad headings of Length and Territory, Rights and Responsibilities plus Renewal, Assignment and Termination – which will naturally differ from one agreement to another – you might expect to see the following basic and equally balanced points, each set out in a clear and reasonable manner. As well as reading through this checklist, you may find it useful to look at the contract reproduced on page 126, with the kind permission of Apollo Window Blinds Ltd.

Length and Territory

• The names and addresses of the franchisor and the franchisee along with the type of work activity being franchised must be stated.

• The franchise ought to exist for a sufficient period of time, usually five to seven years, to enable the franchisee to capitalise fully on his or her total investment.

- A territory should be allocated to the franchisee which is a fair distance – varying according to circumstances – from other franchisees in the network. The franchisee ought to be discouraged from pursuing trade in fellow franchisees' areas, and vice versa.

Rights and Responsibilities

- The franchisor shall permit the franchisee to use his or her trading name, image, systems, procedures, operating manual and so on for the duration of the franchise.

- Ownership of the trading name, image, systems, procedures, operating manual and so forth must reside with the franchisor, who should be entitled to exercise complete control over their usage by the franchisee.

- The franchisee ought to endeavour to the best of his or her abilities to uphold the highest possible standards in every area, by complying with the franchisor's advice and instructions at all times.

- The confidentiality of the trading name, image, systems, procedures, operating manual and so on must be maintained by the franchisee during and after the franchise.

- The (clearly stated) initial fee may be payable in stages, typically on signature of the contract, on delivery of the equipment and machinery and so forth.

- The franchisor could be responsible for choosing a suitable commercial property for the franchisee as well as a territory, handling negotiations, planning permission and so on.

- The franchisor must provide full training for the franchisee, thus enabling him or her to start and properly run the venture. If either party decides during the training programme that the franchisee is unsuited to the franchise, the initial fee ought to be fully refunded less a deduction equal to the franchisor's expenses to date.

- An operating manual covering every possible management and operational topic must be supplied, with updates and amendments regularly and freely added.

- The franchisor should constantly attempt to conceive and develop new and improved systems, procedures and so forth, if and where appropriate. These ought to be tested in his or her own outlets before introducing them to the franchisee at the earliest, safest opportunity. Retraining must take place, when necessary.

- The franchisee should draw any ideas or suggestions for improvements to the franchisor's attention and allow them to be implemented across the whole network.

- The franchisee must devote all of his or her energies to the franchised venture and should not be directly or indirectly involved in the running of any other competitive or non-competitive concern during the term of the franchise.

- The business ought to be operated for an agreed, minimum number of hours, perhaps at certain times. A retail outlet may have to open for 48 hours per week, from 9 to 5 o'clock.

- The franchisee must maintain the commercial premises (if relevant) to an acceptable, specified state of decoration, repair, cleanliness and sanitation to upkeep the reputation and image of the network.

- Stock, equipment and machinery should be purchased only from the franchisor or nominated sources (as appropriate) at prices which are comparable to those in the open market. The franchisee must not buy from other suppliers unless written approval is previously obtained from the franchisor (which should not be withheld if supplies are late or of unacceptably low quality). He or she must not pass on any goods to fellow franchisees (who may be in breach of contract or in dispute with the franchisor).

- The franchisee must ensure that his or her staff conform to the franchisor's well defined selection criteria, are always personally clean, tidily dressed and polite and attentive to customers. All employees should sign an undertaking not to disclose anything about the business to another party during or after their employment.

- Full insurance must be carried by the franchisee at all times, and statutory and other legal obligations should be complied with.

- The franchisee may be obliged to display point of sale material and use other promotional items such as bags and wrapping which bear the franchisor trade name and logo, perhaps supplied by the franchisor at cost prices.

- Regional and national advertising will usually be the responsibility of the franchisor, paid for by the franchisee, possibly through a separate advertising levy. The franchisor must account for advertising expenditure each year. The franchisee should not advertise without the franchisor's consent.

- The franchisee must be entitled to benefit from the franchisor's accumulated knowledge, skills and experience at any time, with regular – or immediate, when necessary – access to experienced trouble-shooters.

- The on-going royalty fee should be carefully stated along with payment arrangements, normally monthly in arrears. No minimum fee should be set.

- The franchisor should be allowed to enter the franchisee's commercial premises at any reasonable time (in practice, trading hours) to see that the terms and conditions of the contract are being honoured.

- Notification of any contractual breaches by the franchisee should be supplied in writing by the franchisor along with details of the corrective steps that need to be taken and a date by which they should be completed, usually two to fourteen days depending on the situation.

- Both the franchisor and the franchisee must share a joint responsibility to try to resolve disputes in good faith and with goodwill, through direct communication and nego tiation.

- An independent arbitration procedure should be established – ideally through the British Franchise Association – to speedily and conveniently remedy disagreements in an equal and amicable manner.

Renewal, Assignment and Termination

- The franchise should be renewable for a further period on the same or similar terms and conditions, assuming that the franchisee is not currently in (and has not previously been in repetitive) breach of the contract. A modest renewal fee, perhaps 10 per cent of the initial fee, may be payable to cover the franchisor's costs.

- The franchisor should normally reserve the first option to buy if or when the franchisee decides to sell his or her franchised venture. If this opportunity is taken up, the concern must be purchased at its current market value, as calculated by a mutually acceptable, independent expert.

- A fair introductory fee – possibly 10 per cent of the selling price – could be charged by the franchisor who performs the role of a business transfer agent by introducing a suitable buyer to the franchisee and subsequently acting as an intermediary for them.

- The franchisor should be entitled to vet a prospective purchaser chosen by the franchisee and be allowed to reject him or her if the usual selection criteria – personality, background and so on – are not wholly met.

- A reasonable transfer fee – perhaps 5 per cent of the selling price – may be demanded from the franchisee who finds his or her own (satisfactory) buyer. This should just cover the franchisor's changeover expenses, for additional training and so forth.

- The franchisee ought to be permitted to terminate the franchise for whatever reason by giving fair written notice – typically three months – and without incurring a financial penalty, except for the loss of his or her initial fee.

- The franchisor should be entitled to terminate (or not renew) the franchise only on the franchisee's insolvency, an irreparable breach of a major term or condition, failure to remedy a breach within a reasonable stipulated period, consistent breaches, business abandonment or a serious criminal offence.

- The franchisor who terminates (or does not allow renewal of) the franchise ought to buy back any assets – equipment, machinery and so on – from the franchisee at their independently assessed market price.

- The franchisee must not use the franchisor's trading name, image, systems, procedures, operating manual and so on following the termination of the franchise. Nor should he or she be able to open a similar venture for a set number of years (usually two) or within a reasonable distance (according to circumstances) of his or her former territory (and premises, if relevant).

- In the event of the franchisee's death during the franchise, his or her successors should be allowed to either assign the business on the same terms and conditions that would have applied to the franchisee or to maintain it as a going concern until one or more of them is suitably qualified to become the new franchisee. Where appropriate, the franchisor should provide temporary management cover at the current market rate.

The text of the contract that appears on the following pages is reproduced with the kind permission of Apollo Window Blinds Limited. The detail of the text is well worth reading as it gives a clear idea of the areas that will become legally binding on franchisees once they agree to join the club, as it were.

FRANCHISE AGREEMENT

BETWEEN:-

APOLLO WINDOW BLINDS LIMITED, incorporated under the Companies Act with registered number 2851496 and having its registered office at Mersey Industrial Estate, Heaton Mersey, Stockport, Cheshire, SK4 3EQ. ("the Franchisor"); and

THE PERSON named as Franchisee in Part I of the Schedule (the "Franchisee").

(A)   The Franchisor is engaged in the business of manufacturing, distributing, merchandising and promoting the sale of window blinds and related products under the name "Apollo Window Blinds" which is operated in accordance with a distinctive system contained in the Manual, a copy of which is annexed to this Agreement.

(B)   A substantial and exclusive reputation and goodwill exists in the name "Apollo Window Blinds", and the Franchisor is the proprietor of the Trade Mark(s) and of the Intellectual Property.

(C)   The Franchisee desires to obtain the benefit of the knowledge, skill and experience of the Franchisor and the right to operate the business system of the Franchisor upon the terms and subject to the Conditions set out in Part III of the Schedule and the Manual.

THEREFORE the parties hereby contract and agree as follows:-

1   **Definitions**

The terms defined in the Conditions shall have the meanings set out therein for the purposes of this Agreement and the Manual.

2   **Condition Precedent**

The Franchisee shall, prior to the Commencement Date, have obtained and shall, with effect from the Commencement Date, throughout the term of this Agreement, hold a valid Value Added Tax Registration in respect of the Franchise granted in terms of this Agreement and shall observe and comply with the terms of the same. The Franchisee hereby acknowledges that any failure by it to hold such a registration during the term of this Agreement shall be deemed to be a material breach of this Agreement and shall result in the termination of this Agreement and shall render the Franchisee liable to indemnify the Franchisor against any and all loss, cost, expenses or damages suffered, whether directly or indirectly as a result of the same.

3   **Franchise**

The Franchisor grants to the Franchisee the exclusive right to operate the Business in the Territory from and at the Premises as principal on the terms of this Agreement, the Conditions and the Manual with effect from the Commencement Date during the Initial Period until terminated in accordance with the Conditions and the Manual.

4   **Premises**

4.1   The parties agree that the Business shall be conducted from the Premises.

4.2   The Premises authorised for the sole purpose of carrying out the Business, in accordance with the terms of this Agreement, are those specified in Part I of the Schedule.

4.3   Prior to the Commencement Date the Franchisor shall procure that the Initial Works required and designed to bring the Premises up to the Franchisor's standards and to properly reflect the Franchisor's corporate identity, shall be completed. The Franchisee shall pay 15% of the agreed start up costs and expenses (including VAT) of the Initial Works to the Franchisor at least 14 days prior to the scheduled opening of the Business, the balance to be paid by the Franchisee on the first day of trading of the Business.

4.4   The Franchisee acknowledges that it shall not alter or convert the Premises upon completion of the Initial Works without the prior written consent of the Franchisor.

4.5   The Franchisee shall not alter or convert the finished Premises in any way without the previous consent in writing of the Franchisor.

4.6   Any alteration or installation to or at the Premises shall be carried out by the Franchisee only in accordance with such plans, drawings and specifications approved by the Franchisor in writing.

4.7   The Franchisee shall fit the Premises with only those fixtures, fittings, equipment and signage specified by the Franchisor.

If for any reason, the Franchisee is required to make changes to the fittings, fixtures or signage of the Premises, such changes will be made within a reasonable period of time as agreed with the Franchisor.

4.8   The Franchisee shall be responsible for complying with all statutory or legal requirements and regulations which apply to the Premises and/or the Business.

4.9   *[The Franchisor and the Franchisee shall enter into a Sub-Lease in respect of the Premises in the form annexed to this Agreement upon [the date of this Agreement]/[completion ofthe Initial Works].]

4.10   *[The Franchisee warrants to the Franchisor that it is the [feu holder]/[freeholder]/[tenant] of the Premises and that it has obtained all necessary consents, permissions and licences to enable the Initial Works to be undertaken and to operate the Business from the Premises. The Franchisee covenants that throughout the continuance of this Agreement it shall observe all statutory and contractual obligations relating to its occupation and use of the Premises and shall not do any act or make any omission which may result in such occupation or usage ceasing.]

5   **Governing Law**

This Agreement shall be governed by the laws of England. The parties hereby submit to the non-exclusive jurisdiction of the British courts.

IN WITNESS WHEREOF these presents consisting of this and the four preceding pages together with the Schedule annexed hereto are executed as follows:-

SUBSCRIBED for and on behalf of the said APOLLO WINDOW BLINDS LIMITED

at

on the   day of   Two thousand and [   ]

by   ....

        (print name)   Director's signature

its Director before the following witness: -

Witness (Sign) ....

Name (Print)   ....

Address   ....

SUBSCRIBED by the said   ....

                                        (print name)   Franchisee's signature

at

on the   day of   Two thousand and [   ]

before the following witness:-

Witness (Sign) ....

Name (Print)   ....

Address   ....

Occupation   ....

THE CONDITIONS

6 **Definitions**

6.1 Unless the context shall otherwise require, the following terms shall have the meanings set opposite them:-

"the Business"	the business of distributing, marketing, offering for sale and selling exclusively the Products, operated and conducted under the Trade Marks using the System more particularly described in the Manual;
"the Commencement Date"	the date specified in Part I of the Schedule;
"the Franchise"	the non-exclusive right granted by the Franchisor to operate the Business by the Franchisee as principal on the terms of this Agreement;
"the Franchisee"	the person specified in Part I of the Schedule as franchisee;
"the Initial Period"	a period of 5 years from the commencement Date;
"the Initial Works"	the installation of the external signs and Shopfittings at the Premises by the Franchisor in terms of the outline specification of works annexed to this Agreement;
"the Manual"	the operations manual (as amended from time to time) provided by the Franchisor and to be adhered to and implemented by the Franchisee in the Business;
"Marketing Material"	the literature, point of sale and marketing material provided by the Franchisor for use in the Business;
"the Permitted Business Name"	Apollo Window Blinds;
"Postcode District"	the geographical areas comprised in the postcode districts as shown in the Postcode Atlas published by Bartholomew (an imprint of Harper Collins publishers);
"the Premises"	the premises specified in Part I of the Schedule for the operation of the Business by the Franchisee;
"the Products"	all types of window blinds and related products manufactured and sold under the name "Apollo Window Blinds" as specified in the Manual;
"the Shopfittings"	those fixtures and fittings external and internal to be situated at the Premises and authorised by the Franchisor other than such items as form part of the fabric ofthe building;
"the System"	the distinctive business format and method developed by the Franchisor in connection with the operation of the Business utilising and comprising the Trade Marks and certain standard operational procedures, plans, directions, specifications, methods, management and advertising techniques and identification schemes, part of which are contained in the Manual;
"Territory"	the postcode districts more particularly described in Part I of the Schedule;
"Trade Marks"	the trade marks the particulars of which are set out in Part II of the Schedule; and
"Training Period"	a period of [ ] from the Commencement Date.

6.2 Save as expressly provided for, references in this Agreement to this Agreement or any other document are to this Agreement or such other document as varied, supplemented, novated and/or replaced in any manner from time to time.

6.3. Reference to Clauses and Schedules are to be construed as references to clauses, and schedules of this Agreement unless otherwise stated.

6.4. The headings in this Agreement are inserted for ease of reference only and shall not affect its construction.

7 **Appointment**

7.1 The Franchisor hereby appoints the Franchisee as its exclusive distributor in the Territory and grants to the Franchisee the exclusive right to market, distribute, supply and sell within the Territory the Products purchased from the Franchisor on the terms and conditions contained in this Agreement, these Conditions and the Manual. The Franchisee acknowledges that the Franchisor shall be entitled to amend or vary the Manual at any time and the Franchisee shall be bound by such amendments and variations. In the event of any conflict between the terms of this Agreement and the Manual, the terms of the Manual shall prevail.

7.2 The Franchisor further grants the Franchisee the rights to use the Permitted Business Name and the Trade Marks at the Premises in connection with the Business. The Franchisee is not permitted to use the Permitted Business Name or the Trade Marks or any deviation of the same in any manner which has not been authorised in writing by the Franchisor. The Franchisee may not use the Permitted Business Name or the Trade Marks in any corporate name.

7.3 On the date of execution of this Agreement, the Franchisor shall deliver one copy of the Manual to the Franchisee. For the avoidance of doubt, the Franchisee hereby acknowledges that the Manual shall be and remain the sole property of the Franchisor, and the Franchisee shall not be entitled to make any copies of the Manual.

7.4 The Franchisee agrees that it will not make any use of and will not permit or authorise any use directly or indirectly of the System or the Trade Marks by any third party.

7.5 The Franchisee shall not actively sell the Products outside the Territory and will not knowingly offer or provide any information or assistance concerning the System or the Trade Marks to any person, firm or undertaking who intends or may seek to use or resell them outside the Territory.

7.6 For the avoidance of doubt, nothing contained in this Agreement shall be construed as a restriction upon the Franchisor from marketing, distributing or supplying any products not covered by this Agreement in the Territory, whether to the Franchisee's customers or otherwise.

7.7 The Franchisee shall not hold itself out as the Franchisor's agent for sales of the Products or as being entitled to bind the Franchisor in any way, provided always that the Franchisee shall be entitled to describe itself as a franchise or as authorised franchisee of the Business and as such the distributor and supplier of the Products.

7.8 The Franchisee shall not sell any of the Products which it purchases from the Franchisor through sales agents or to a sub-distributor without the prior written consent of the Franchisor.

7.9 For the avoidance of doubt, all of the Franchisee's operating expenses, including the expense of maintaining business premises, shall be for the Franchisee's account.

8 **Duration**

8.1 The Agreement shall commence on the Commencement Date and subject to the provisions of Condition 8 shall continue for the Initial Period.

8.2 The Franchise may thereafter be extended at the option of the Franchisee and with the Franchisor's consent for a further period of 5 years commencing on the day following the date of expiry of the Initial Period subject to the following:-

8.2.1 the service on the Franchisor of a notice signed by the Franchisee not later than six calendar months prior to expiry of the Initial Period; and

8.2.2 throughout the Initial Period there has been proper performance by the Franchisee of all its obligations hereunder and there having been no material breach by the Franchisee of the terms of this Agreement entitling the Franchisor to terminate this Agreement under the provision of Condition 8 either at the date of giving notice to the Franchisor under Condition 3.2.1 above or at the expiration of such notice; and

8.2.3   execution by the Franchisee of a new agreement in the standard form used by the Franchisor at the time of service of the notice referred to in Condition 3.2.1; and

8.2.4   the Franchisee having previously undertaken in writing to carry out such works of renovation, modernisation and refurbishment to the Premises and to replacement of such fixtures, signs, furnishings and equipment as are specified to the Franchisee by the Franchisor prior to the date of renewal and reasonably necessary to bring the Premises up to the then current standards of design and decor of the System or to comply with any statutory requirements or regulations relating to public health and safety, all at the Franchisee's expenses.

9   **Franchisee's Obligations**

9.1   The Franchisee agrees at all times during the continuance of this Agreement:-

9.1.1   to commence, establish and maintain the Business at the Premises from the Commencement Date;

9.1.2   to operate the Business strictly in accordance with and to conform in all respects and at all times with the provisions ofthe Manual;

9.1.3   to use its best endeavours to establish, maintain and maximise the turnover of the Business;

9.1.4   to pay all sums specified in the Manual in accordance with the procedures specified in the Manual;

9.1.5   to carry on only the Business at the Premises and not to carry on any other business whatsoever at the Premises or permit the sale therefrom of any goods other than the Products;

9.1.6   to offer for sale the Franchisor's complete range of Products;

9.1.7   to obtain all the Products from the Franchisor or its approved suppliers;

9.1.8   not to make use of or disclose any information or knowledge about the materials and the specifications of the Products for any purpose nor make any copies of them either before or after termination of this Agreement;

9.1.9   to provide and maintain the agreed service levels for the Business, and not to sell any product nor provide any service which does not conform to the standards specified by the Franchisor;

9.1.10   to comply with all reasonable instructions given by the Franchisor with regard to the standard or quality of service to be provided by the Franchisee;

9.1.11   to provide the following services to its customers:

9.1.11.1. to measure and quote, without charge, by suitably qualified staff attending promptly at the residence or business premises in which the Products are to be installed or delivered without any obligation upon the prospective customer to purchase;

9.1.11.2. to install or deliver any Products purchased by the customer by suitably qualified staff attending promptly;

9.1.11.3. to provide after sales service by suitably qualified staff attending promptly, to ensure trouble free performance of the Products supplied and to repair and/or replace any Products which are bona fide defective;

9.1.12.   to maintain, (with a reputable insurance company approved by the Franchisor), adequate insurance cover against loss (including loss of profits) or damage arising from fire, explosion, impact, burglary and such other risks in the minimum sums as agreed with the Franchisor from time to time, against all liability (including Product liability) of the Franchisor, Franchisee and any supplier of the Franchisee, to the Franchisee's employees and customers and additionally, public liability insurance to the value of £5 million;

9.1.13   not to engage in any activities at the Premises, which may be contrary to any legislation or regulations imposed by any competent authority. The Franchisor may by notice in writing specify any matter or thing required to be done or omitted to be done to ensure that such legislation or regulations are complied with and upon such notice the Franchisee shall immediately do or omit to do the same;

9.1.14   to protect and promote the goodwill attaching to the Business, the Permitted Business Name, the Trade Marks and the use of the System. The Franchisee shall not do anything, which would or might bring the name of the Franchisor, the Trade Marks, the Permitted Business Name or the System into disrepute. The Franchisee shall notify the Franchisor immediately of any occurrence or fact which has affected or could adversely affect the value thereof, and shall take such reasonable action as the Franchisor may direct;

9.1.15   not to use the Permitted Business Name or Trade Marks for any purpose other than in relation to the Business and in accordance with the Manual;

9.1.16   to diligently carry on the Business at the Premises and use its best endeavours to seek, establish and develop sales of the Products within the Territory,

9.1.17   not to actively market or canvas or promote the Business outwith the Territory without the prior written authority of the Franchiser;

9.1.18   to enter into a registered user agreement in such form and with such person as is required by the Franchisor in respect of the Trade Marks;

9.1.19   not to pledge the credit of the Franchisor not to represent itself as being the Franchisor or agent or partner of the Franchiser;

9.1.20   to keep confidential the System and the contents of the Manual and the terms of this Agreement;

9.1.21   at the Franchisee's own expense to obtain and maintain in force all consents, licences and permissions necessary for the operation of the Business and the exhibition of advertising signs and other matters at the Premises and to comply with all rules, regulations and by-laws of the relevant authorities relating thereto;

9.1.22   to apply for and maintain in force a Consumer Credit Licence (at the Franchisee's own expense) via the Office of Fair Trading and to lodge a copy with the Franchiser within no more than three months of the Commencement Date;

9.1.23   to deliver to the Franchiser within seven days after the due date for submission to H.M. Customs and Excise a copy of the Franchisee's return and a copy of any assessment raised against it by H.M. Customs and Excise; and

9.1.24   forthwith to give notice by facsimile followed by written confirmation of any legal process, whether criminal or civil, served, received or levied at the Premises or upon the Franchisee and whether in relation to the Business or otherwise and to provide to the Franchisor such further information as the Franchisor may require in connection therewith.

10   **Franchisor's Obligations**

10.1   The Franchisor shall allocate a geographical territory in which the Franchisee will actively market and promote the Business in the Territory. Such Territory shall be as defined in Part I of the Schedule.

10.2   The Franchisor agrees at all times during the continuance of this Agreement:-

10.2.1   to act reasonably wherever the Franchisor is required in terms of this Agreement or the Manual to give its consent or take any decision relative to the Franchisee;

10.2.2   to sell the Products to the Franchisee at the Franchisor's standard trade price list, as published and revised from time to time; and

10.2.3   to inform the Franchisee in writing of any proposed alterations to the System.

11   **Payment**

11.1   The Franchisee shall pay all sums due by the Franchisee to the Franchisor pursuant to this Agreement or the Manual in accordance with the terms of this Agreement and the Manual.

11.2   In the event of any default in payment on the due date of any due sum, the Franchisor will, in addition to any other remedies available to it, suspend the supplies of Products and services until payment is made.

Further, in the event of any default in the payment of sums due, the Franchisor shall have the right to charge interest at the rate of 2% per month calculated on a day to day basis on the amount of any sums outstanding from the above date of payment as specified in this Agreement or the Manual until settlement, both before and after payment.

12 Restrictions

12.1 The Franchisee agrees that during the continuance of this Agreement and for one year after its termination it shall not, whether as principal, servant, agent or as director or shareholder in any company or in any other capacity, and whether alone or jointly with any other person, firm or corporation:-

12.1.1 carry on or be involved in either directly or indirectly any business competitive or in conflict . with the Business within or within a radius of three quarters of a mile from the Postcode District or any other premises at which a business is carried on under the Permitted Business Name;

12.1.2 approach or endeavour to employ or engage, any employee of the Franchisor or any person to whom the Franchisor has made an offer of employment, or any person employed by or who has been made such an offer by any other holder of a franchise granted by the Franchisor;

12.1.3 interfere with, solicit or entice any customer of the Business (meaning any person who has regularly or habitually purchased Products from the Franchisee within the period of one year prior to such termination) with the intent that he cease to deal with the Business or any successor to the Business of the Franchisee at the Premises.

12.2 Upon termination of this Agreement the Franchisee shall cease use of the Trade Marks and the Permitted Business Name and shall not use any name which resembles that name or may reasonably be confused with it and not in any way to suggest any continuing connection or association with the Business or the Franchisor.

13 Assignation

13.1 The Franchisee shall not assign the benefit of all or any part of this Agreement without the previous written consent of the Franchisor which shall not be unreasonably withheld.

13.2 The assignation of the benefit of this Agreement is subject to payment of the Franchisor's legal costs plus VAT thereon relating to such consent and the preparation of such documentation as may be required in relation thereto.

13.3 The application for the Franchisor's consent to assign the benefit of this Agreement ("the Application") shall state the name and address of the proposed assignee and the purchase price (if any) to be paid by the proposed assignee ("the Price").

13.4 On receipt of the Application the Franchisor may by serving notice in writing served within 28 days of receipt of the Application elect to purchase the Business at the Price.

13.5 Any failure by the Franchisor to exercise its right shall be without prejudice to its right to refuse its consent to any proposed assignation but in the event that the Franchisor does grant its consent to any proposed assignation such assignation shall take place only to the proposed assignee and for the Price and on the other terms specified in the Application.

13.6 Any advertisement relating to the proposed assignation of the benefit of this Agreement shall be made only in such form and at such location or in such newspaper, periodical or other publication as shall be agreed by the Franchisor in writing but in any event no notice or advertisement whatsoever in relation thereto shall be placed on the exterior or within the Premises.

14 Summary Termination

14.1 The Franchisor may terminate this Agreement forthwith by written notice to that effect to the Franchisee if:-

14.1.1 during the Training Period it becomes apparent to the Franchisor that the Franchisee does not meet the Franchisor's requirements and standards;

14.1.2 the Franchisee shall have failed to observe or perform any of the obligations of this

Agreement. If any such failure is capable of remedy the Franchisee shall have a period of 30 days to remedy the breach from receipt of notice requiring its remedy. Failure to observe or perform any of the obligations in the Manual shall constitute a breach;

14.1.3 the Franchisee shall become insolvent by way of inability to pay its debts or shall enter into liquidation whether voluntarily or compulsory or shall make any arrangement or composition with its creditors or shall have a receiver or administrator appointed over all or part of its assets or shall take or suffer any similar action in consequence of a debt;

14.1.4 the Franchisee shall cease for whatever reason to be entitled to occupy the Premises and shall be unable to find alternative premises within the Territory deemed, in the reasonable opinion of the Franchisor, to be suitable for theBusiness within a period of 3 months.

14.1.5 in the event that there is a change in any of the shareholders in the Franchisee from the shareholders at the date of this Agreement the Franchisee shall immediately notify the Franchisor in writing of such change. The Franchisor shall have the right to terminate this Agreement forthwith for a period of six (6) months from the date of such notice.

14.1.6 the personal representatives of a deceased Franchisee shall not have completed an assignment of the benefit of this agreement in accordance with the provisions of Condition 6 within a period of six months calculated from the date of the death of the Franchisee.

14.2 This Agreement will terminate automatically in the event that the Franchisee becomes de-registered for Value Added Tax with H.M. Customs & Excise during the term of this Agreement. For the avoidance of doubt such de-registration shall constitute a breach of this Agreement.

15 Intellectual Property

15.1 The Franchisor hereby authorises the Franchisee to use the Trade Marks in the Territory on or in relation to the Products for the purposes only of exercising its rights and performing its obligations under this Agreement.

15.2 The Franchisee shall ensure that each reference to and use of any of the Trade Marks by the Franchisee is in a manner from time to time approved by the Franchisor and accompanied by an acknowledgement, in a form approved by the Franchisor, that the same is a trade mark (or registered trade mark) of the Franchisor.

15.3 The Franchisee shall not:

15.3.1 make any modifications to the Products without prior written consent of the Franchisor;

15.3.2 alter or remove or tamper with any Trade Marks, numbers or other means of identification used on or in relation to the Products;

15.3.3 use any of the Trade Marks in any way which might prejudice their distinctiveness or validity or the goodwill of the Franchisor herein;

15.3.4 use in relation to the Products any trade marks other than the Trade Marks without obtaining the prior written consent of the Franchisor;

15.3.5 use in the Territory any trade marks or trade names so resembling any trade marks or trade names of the Franchisor including the Trade Marks as to be likely to cause confusion or deception; or

15.3.6 change, mutilate, obscure or otherwise deface or interfere with any service mark, trade name, Trade Mark or other information appearing on the Products.

15.4 Except as provided in Condition 8.1 of this Agreement the Franchisee shall have no rights in respect of any trade names or Trade Marks used by the Franchisor in relation to the Products or of the goodwill associated therewith, and the Franchisee hereby acknowledges that, except as expressly provided in this Agreement, it shall not acquire any rights in respect thereof and that all such rights and goodwill are, and shall remain, vested in the Franchisor.

15.5 For the avoidance of doubt, the Franchisee hereby acknowledges that the Shop fittings and the layout of the Premises form part of the intellectual property rights of the Franchisor and the Franchisee shall not alter, remove, tamper, change or otherwise interfere with the same except as expressly permitted in writing by the Franchisor.

15.6 The Franchisee shall, at the expense of the Franchisor, take all such steps as the Franchisor may reasonably require to assist the Franchisor in maintaining the validity and enforceability of the intellectual property of the Franchisor including the Trade Marks, during the term of this Agreement.

15.7 The Franchisee shall promptly and fully notify the Franchisor of any actual, threatened or suspected infringement in the Territory of any of the intellectual property of the Franchisor including, without limiting the foregoing generality, the Trade Marks which comes to the Franchisee's notice, and any claim by any third party so coming to its notice that the sale of the Products within the Territory infringes any rights of any other person, and the Franchisee shall at the request and expense of the Franchisor do all such things as may be reasonably required to assist the Franchisor in taking or resisting anyproceedings in relation to any such infringement or claim.

15.8 Nothing contained in this Agreement shall entitle the Franchisee to take any action in respect of the infringement of the Trade Marks or any other intellectual property which is owned by the Franchisor, without the prior written consent of the Franchisor.

15.9 The Franchisor gives no warranty to the Franchisee that the use or sale by it of the Products will not infringe the intellectual property rights of any third party and under no circumstances shall the Franchisor be liable to indemnify the Franchisee with regard to any loss, cost, injury or damage incurred or suffered by the Franchisee in respect of any such infringement.

16 **Force Majeure**

Both parties shall be released from their obligations hereunder in the event that national emergency, war, prohibitive government regulations or any other cause beyond the control of either party shall render performance of this Agreement economically enviable for a period in excess of 3 consecutive months whereupon all amounts incurred due and payable shall be paid immediately and the Franchisee shall forthwith cease the operation of the Business at the Premises.

17 **Procedure on Termination**

Upon expiry or termination ofthis Agreement:

17.1 The Franchisee will forthwith procure the transfer of the telephone number used at the Premises to the Franchisor or its nominee;

17.2 All rights of the Franchisee pursuant to this Agreement shall cease and determine absolutely save that the restrictions contained in Condition 5 shall continue in full force and effect;

17.3 The Franchisee will within 72 hours of receipt of notice of any termination deliver to the Franchisor a list of all customers of the Business and their telephone numbers and a list of persons employed by the Franchisee in the Business with full details including names, home addresses~ employment position, date of birth, salary and other emoluments, and date of commencement of employment by the Franchisee;

17.4 The Franchisee will vacate the Premises and remove all the Franchisee's and any third party's property and effects from the Premises forthwith causing no damage, and in default of so going by or on the date of termination the Franchisor may procure the removal of the same from the Premises at the sole cost of the Franchisee;

17.5 The Franchisee will return to the Franchisor all copies of the Manual and the Marketing Material and shall not retain any copies.

18 **Indemnity**

The Franchisee shall indemnify and hold the Franchisor harmless from any loss, cost, damage or expense or any liability which it may incur, either directly or indirectly, as a result of or in connection with the use of the Products or the sale of the Products or the operation of the Business by the Franchisee or any third party where such loss, cost, damage, expense or liability is the result of an act or omission on the part of the Franchisee. The Franchisee shall also indemnify and hold the Franchisor harmless from any loss, cost, damage or expense or any liability which it may incur as a result of any breach by the Franchisee of this Agreement. The provisions of this Condition shall survive termination of this Agreement.

19 **General**

19.1 It is expressly agreed and declared:-

19.1 the expiration or termination of this Agreement shall be without prejudice to the rights of either party accrued prior to the date of such termination or expiration;

19.2 nothing in this Agreement shall constitute a joint venture, agency or partnership or relationship of employer and employee between the Franchisor and the Franchisee; and

19.3 in the event that any provision clause, sub-clause or part thereof of this Agreement or these Conditions shall be void, voidable or illegal, the Franchisor may at its sole discretion sever or amend such provision in such manner as renders the remainder of this Agreement or these conditions enforceable and this Agreement shall not determine.

20 **Notices**

Any notice required or authorised to be given under this Agreement may be served by pre-paid registered letter or facsimile transmission addressed to the party in question at the address contained in this Agreement or to such other address as may be notified in writing by that party to the other party for the purposes of this Agreement. Any notice so given by letter shall be deemed to have been served 72 hours after it shall have been posted and by facsimile upon the date of transmission. In proving service it shall be sufficient in the case of a registered letter to produce the receipt of the post office therefor and in the case of a facsimile message to produce a copy of such message together with the facsimile activity report timed and dated and bearing the facsimile number of the addressee.

Key Facts

Both the franchisor and the would-be franchisee must seek help and guidance from a solicitor who is fully experienced in the franchise market, prior to signing a mutually binding franchise agreement.

The franchise contract should be complete, clear and equally fair to the two parties. The duration of the agreement, the territory allocated to the franchisee, the respective rights and responsibilities and the terms and conditions of renewing, assigning and terminating the contract should be spelled out.

9

WORKING AS A TEAM

The franchisor and franchisee partnership is an unusual one, with two completely independent businesses joined together and each dependent on the other for their continued well being. If your own particular union is to be both personally and financially rewarding, you must understand the complexities of the ever-changing relationship and be aware of the potential problems and pitfalls that may arise. Also, you need to know how to make the most of your partnership, either by avoiding these difficulties or resolving them as quickly and as amicably as possible.

Understanding the relationship

Although you and your new partner will be totally ethical – assuming that you chose them in a careful and correct manner and have thus teamed up with the right party – your relationship will almost inevitably still evolve along familiar (and possibly destructive) franchising lines. It has often been likened to that of a parent and child, and appropriately so. There are many similarities, with the parent nurturing the child who changes into an (occasionally) unhappy and rebellious teenager before turning into a mature and responsible adult.

In the early days, the worldly-wise franchisor does almost everything for the inexperienced franchisee; either directly, by finding a site, supplying fixtures, fittings and stock, advertising and promoting, training, researching, developing and updating the format, retraining and so on; or indirectly, by providing systems and procedures, an operating manual, individual advice when necessary and so forth. The franchisor leads, suggesting and coaxing rather than demanding and ordering. The franchisee follows, listening and learning all of the way.

Over the months and years, the balance of the relationship begins to shift and subtly alter. The franchisor continues to beaver away behind the scenes, conducting research and making adjustments whenever relevant. Hands-on help and guidance tend to lessen noticeably though, as the franchisee masters the systems and procedures, knows the products and services well and has successfully operated the format day in and day out at grass roots level for some time.

It is now that problems begin to appear, even between model franchisors and franchisees in well matched relationships. Naturally, the franchisee will have his or her own strongly held views based on recent practical experiences and will want ideas, suggestions and criticisms to be heard, taken into account and acted upon, when valid. Should they not be, he or she will become disillusioned, angry and bitter; hardly conducive to continued co-operation and success. Conscious of their undoubted hard work, half believing that they are wholly responsible for their achievements and often unaware of many of the franchisor's ongoing activities, they also start to feel unhappy about paying over royalties every month or so. Again, a recipe for impending disaster.

These difficulties are exacerbated by the simultaneous increase in franchisee numbers, as the franchisor issues more franchises across the country. With added demands on manpower and financial resources, he or she is typically inclined to leave established franchises to stand alone on their own two feet, believing that they will welcome even looser control and fewer check-ups. Without doubt, they will – but they still want to feel that the franchisor is around and they have not been completely cut off and neglected.

Making the Most of Your Partnership

All of these problems – which have destroyed many franchise relationships – may be sidestepped or swiftly rectified if you communicate properly, both making a conscious effort to keep in close and regular contact, to face and work through problems to your mutual advantage. The franchisor's field and head office staff, franchise newsletters and franchisee advisory committees (also called franchisee councils) can play vitally significant roles in improving and sustaining your partnership.

Those trouble-shooting field operatives who provide onsite opening assistance, call in to check guidelines are being followed, supply on-the-spot retraining and advice as required, and who recognise management and operating difficulties before they have become fully apparent, should act as intermediaries. Planned developments, forthcoming training programmes, advertising campaigns and so on should be explained and discussed. Constructive ideas, suggestions and experiences must be passed to and fro between the franchisee, franchisor and other franchisees in the area. Even as the network multiplies, the weekly, fortnightly or – more likely – monthly visits should be retained with in-between telephone calls to warm the atmosphere, build loyalty and strengthen personal ties.

Individually experienced in their various specialist topics such as equipment installation and usage, staff recruitment and so on, the head office team must each be known and readily available to the franchisee – they must not be just a list of names hidden away in the back pages of a manual. Meeting all of them when first visiting the premises, possessing their telephone extension numbers and being contacted by the appropriate person when a specific query cannot be immediately solved by the trouble-shooter, will all help the franchisee and further cement the partnership.

A monthly newsletter is a good idea. It can perhaps start off as a single sided, typed and photocopied sheet and slowly transform into a fully-fledged magazine as the network expands. Details of the franchisor's recent and proposed actions, information concerning new franchisees, news about existing franchisees' activities, successes and failures, wide-ranging articles and letters from the franchisor's field and head office staff and franchisees, news and reviews of events such as exhibitions and press coverage – all build a corporate identity and foster a healthy team spirit. As an example, a recent edition (Winter 1999/2000) of a newsletter published by Travail Employment Group contained a lively selection of articles all of particular interest to readers, including the following.

- A summarised article from the Financial Times asserting that 'full employment may be close' – a matter of particular importance in the recruitment business.
- Some useful quotes garnered from a recent recruitment exhibition
- Details of the Andover Employee of the Year, who won a spectacular prize holiday courtesy of Travail.
- Statistics taken from the national press illustrating trends in employment and trade.
- Listings of the company's top ten offices.
- Graphical analyses of the Group's daily sales and gross margins with useful explanatory details offering guidance for forecasting future trends.
- Relevant quotes from competitor firms which gave the Travail Group cause for a certain degree of self-satisfaction.
- A statement from an Area Franchise Manager about her personal pleasure in progressing through the ranks and the satisfaction that she derives from her work - very encouraging for new recruits.
- Illustrated examples of forthcoming marketing materials.
- An explanatory article about the setting up of the Recruitment and Employment Federation.
- And, of course, the Company's best wishes to all franchisees and their staffs for the New Millennium.

This approach, presented in colour and with a very appealing layout, encourages all readers and creates a strong and realistic link between the Group's Corporate Centre and its country-wide franchises.

A franchisee advisory committee must be set up by the franchisor and should be well established by the time the chain of outlets reaches double figures. Run as an open forum for the two-way exchange of information, discussion and lively debate, it ought to have an informal constitution, with relaxed quarterly meetings perhaps on the franchisor's premises, if appropriate. These should be attended by everyone – franchisor, field and head office staff and franchisees. As the network grows, it may be necessary to have regional franchisee meetings with representatives being sent to talk and liaise with the franchisor, reporting back in due course.

Key Facts

The unusual franchisor and franchisee relationship where two independent yet entwined concerns work together for mutual success, is comparable in many ways to that of a parent and child.

Any problems which exist within the franchisor/franchisee partnership can usually be averted or remedied by improved communications through troubleshooters, the head office team, newsletters and franchisee councils.

10

LOOKING FORWARD

However happy and lucrative your working relationship with your franchise partner may be – and it ought to be excellent in every respect if you are each completely dedicated to the union – you will still want to grow and expand your own business in due course. The franchisor will seek to take on more franchisees, further building up the network. The franchisee will probably buy other franchises from the franchisor, opening new outlets. If successful growth is to occur, both parties need to review constantly their approach to franchising, spotting errors and implementing changes before moving on either to recruit the next franchisee or purchase another franchise. Only by looking back and learning from the past can you look forward and continue to be a winner.

The Franchisor's Checklist

The franchisor must regularly contemplate the following questions, taking any necessary steps to ensure that his or her answers are all positive, prior to any planned expansion.

- Are you aware of the characteristics of a reputable franchise?

- Does your franchise possess these features?

- Do you know about the different types of franchise available?

- Are you fully familiar with the changing franchise market?

- Does it remain an appealing, long-term prospect for you?

- Do you recognise the main benefits and drawbacks of franchising, along with their respective side effects?

- Do the pros outweigh the cons in your circumstances?

- Are you and your team experienced, ethical, financially sound and committed?

- Is your format proven, distinctive, complete and simple?

- Is your product and service range varied, well established and selling steadily at premium prices?

- Is the market large and growing?

- Are the financial costs and returns manageable and worthwhile?

- Can your quantitative and qualitative objectives best be achieved via this trading method?

- Does your franchise consultant play a key role in your franchising activities?

- Are you still running pilot operations for testing purposes?

- Is your trading name appropriate?

- Have you a first-class image and accumulated goodwill?

- Are your systems and procedures relevant and up to date?

- Do you offer the correct blend of prompt and efficient initial services?

- Is your front-end fee fair and non-profit making?

- Do you provide the right mix of ongoing services in a swift and proper manner?

- Is the operating manual detailed, clear and up to date?

- Is the continuing management service fee reasonable for both parties?

- Is associate (or full) membership of the British Franchise Association of benefit to you?

- Are you promoting the franchise package through the most appropriate sources?

- Are you supplying enough data to allow readers to decide whether you are well suited, and if it is worthwhile requesting further information?

- Is your franchise prospectus informing and attracting suitable would-be franchisees whilst dissuading unsuitable ones from applying?

- Does your franchise application form enable you to properly assess applicants?

- Do you know the types of personality, background, finances and goals that ought to be possessed by the ideal franchisee?

- Are you meeting candidates at their home and your head office, and asking revealing questions?

- Are you choosing the right franchisees?

- Do you liaise with an appropriately experienced solicitor before signing a franchise contract?

- Is the franchise agreement complete, clear and balanced?

- Is the franchise for a sufficient period of time?

- Are your territories evenly spread out?

- Are the rights and responsibilities fair?

- Are the terms and conditions of renewal, assignment and termination all reasonable?

- Do you fully understand the franchisor-franchisee relationship, recognising the franchisee's views?

- Do you communicate with each other at all times, exchanging ideas, suggestions and constructive criticisms?

- Do you regularly review your franchising approach, to maximise your chances of a successful future?

The Franchisee's Checklist

Similarly, the franchisee must continually think about the following queries and should be certain that his or her replies are all favourable, before any proposed growth:

- Do you know the features of an ethical franchise?

- Do you own a reputable franchise?

- Are you familiar with the various types of franchise which exist?

- Do you know the franchise industry well?

- Does it offer you an attractive, viable future?

- Are you aware of the major advantages and disadvantages of franchising, and their individual knock-on effects?

- Do the pluses exceed the minuses for you?

- Are you independent, self-disciplined, ambitious, sociable and trustworthy?

- Are you familiar with the territory, in good health and supported by your loved ones?

- Do you have sufficient money available?

- Are your personal and business goals compatible with franchising?

- Is the franchisor fully knowledgeable, totally reputable, financially secure and in possession of appropriate franchising objectives?

- Is the format completely tried and tested, distinguished, comprehensive and straightforward?

- Are the goods selling well, within a growing marketplace?

- Does the franchise package provide value for money for you?

- Does it also produce a satisfactory return on your investment?

- Is the network wholly successful?

- Is this franchise right for you?

- Do you take relevant professional advice prior to signing any binding agreement?

- Is the franchise contract fair and reasonable?

- Is the franchise long enough for you?

- Is your territory sufficiently profitable for you?

- Are you happy with each party's rights and responsibilities?

- Are the renewal, assignment and termination clauses all even handed?

- Are you aware of the ways in which the franchisor/ franchisee partnership usually develops, sympathising with the franchisor's position?

- Do you get on well with the franchisor, having an open, communicative relationship?

- Do you often conduct a rigorous self-appraisal, to increase the prospects of your future success?

Key Facts

Both the franchisor and franchisee will naturally wish to expand, by recruiting more franchisees and taking on new franchises respectively.

If their expansion is to be a success, the two parties ought to continually reflect upon their franchising approach to date, making improvements as and where necessary.

PART FOUR: THE APPENDICES

APPENDIX A: FRANCHISE ASSOCIATIONS

Franchisors Association of Australia, GPO Box 1498N, Melbourne, Victoria 3001, Australia, Tel: 00 61 3 9650 1667, Fax: 00 61 3 9650 1713

Austrian Franchise Association*, Bayerhamerstrasse 12/1.Stock, 5020 Salzburg, Austria, Tel: 00 43 662 874236-9, Fax: 00 43 662 87422365-5

Belgian Franchise Association*, Bd De L'Humanitie 116/2, 1070 Brussels, Belgium. Tel: 00 32 2 523 97 07, Fax: 00 32 2 523 35 10

Brazilian Franchise Association, Alameda Irae, 276 Moenna, Sao Paulo, Brazil CEP 04027 000, TEl: 00 55 11 571-1303/573-9496, Fax: 00 55 11 575-5590

British Franchise Association*, Thames View, Newtown Road, Henley on Thames, Oxon, RG9 IHG. Tel: 01491 578 050, Fax: 01491 573 517

Canadian Franchise Association, 5045 Orbitor Drive, Building 121, Unit 210, Mississauga, Ontario, Canada, L4W 4Y4, Tel: 00 1 416 625 2896 Fax: 00 1 416 625 9076

Czech Franchise Association*, Rytirska 18-20, 110 00 Prag 1, Czech Republic, Tel/Fax: 00 42 2 224 230 566

Danish Franchise Association*, Maglebjergvej 5 B-D, DK-2800 Lyngby, Denmark, Tel: 00 45 45 88 77 18, Fax: 00 45 45 93 83 41

European Franchise Federation*, Bd De L'Humanitie 116/2, 1070 Brussels, Belgium. Tel: 00 32 2 520 16 07, Fax: 00 32 2 520 17 35

Finnish Franchise Association*, Laurinkatu 47, 08100 Lohja, Finland, Tel: 00 358 19 331 195 Fax: 00 358 19 331 075

French Franchise Association*, 60 Rue la Boetie, 75008 Paris, France, Tel: 00 33 1 53 75 22 25 Fax: 00 33 1 53 75 22 20

German Franchise Association*, Paul-Heyse-Strasse 33-35, 80336 Munich, Germany, Tel: 00 49 89 53 07 14-0, Fax: 00 49 89 53 13 23

Franchise Association of Greece*, Skoufou 10, 105 57 Athens, Greece, Tel: 00 30 1 32 34 620, Fax; 00 30 1 32 38 865

Hong Kong Franchise Association, 22/F United Centre, 95 Queensway, Hong Kong, Tel: 00 852 2823 1225, Fax: 00 852 2527 9843

Hungarian Franchise Association*, c/o DASY, PO Box 446, Budapest H-1536, Hungary, Tel: 00 361 212 4124, Fax: 00 361 212 5712

International Franchise Association, 1350 New York Avenue NW #900, Washington DC 20005, USA. Tel: 00 1 202 628 8000, Fax: 00 1 202 628 0812

Irish Franchise Association, 102 Pembroke Road, Dublin 4, Ireland, Tel: 00 353 1 668 5444, Fax: 00 353 1 668 5541

Israel Franchise Association, Corex Building, Maskit Street, Herzlia Pituach 46733, Israel, Tel: 00 972 52 576 631, Fax: 00 972 52 572 580

Italian Franchising Association*, Corso di Porto Nuova 3, 20121 Milan, Italy. Tel: 00 390 2 2900 37 79, Fax: 00 390 2 655 59 19

Japanese Franchise Association, Elsa Building 602, 3-13-12 Rippongi, Minato-ku, Tokyo, Japan, Tel: 00 81 3 3401 0421, Fax: 00 81 3 3423 2019

Mexican Franchise Association, Insurgentes Sur 1783 no 303, Colonia Guadeloupe Inn, Mexico City 01020, Mexico, Tel: 00 52 5 255 45 57, Fax: 00 52 5 661 0655

Netherlands Franchise Association*, Boomberglaan 12, 1217 RR Hilversum, The Netherlands, Tel: 00 31 35 624 23 00, Fax: 00 31 35 624 91 94

New Zealand Franchise Association, PO Box 25 650, St Heliers Bay, Auckland, New Zealand, Tel: 00 64 9 575 3804, Fax: 00 64 9 575 3807

Norwegian Franchise Association, PO Box 2900, Oslo 0230, Norway, Tel: 00 47 2 55 82 20, Fax: 00 47 2 55 82 25

Polish Franchise Association*, 1 Szpitalna Street, II Floor Room 5, 00-020 Warsaw, Poland, Tel: 00 48 22/26 80 30 39 Ext 120, Tel/fax 00 48 2 625 6956

Portuguese Franchise Association*, Rua Viriato 25 3, 1050 Lisbon, Portugal, Tel: 00 351 1 315 18 45, Fax: 00 351 1 54 22 20

Romanian Franchise Association*, Bd Aviatorilor 86, Sector 1, Bucharest, Romania, Tel: 00 40 1 223 1893, Fax: 00 40 1 223 2307

Slovenian Franchise Association, Dimiceva 13, 1504 Ljubljana, Slovenia, Tel: 00 286 61 16 82 331, Fax: 00 386 61 16 82 775

Spanish Franchise Association*, Avenida de las Ferias s/n, Apda 476, 46035 Valencia, Spain, Tel: 00 34 96 386 11 23, Fax: 00 34 96 363 61 11

Franchise Association of Southern Africa, Postnet Suite 267, Private Bag X30500, 2041 Houghton, Republic of South Africa, Tel: 00 27 11 484 1285, Fax: 00 27 11 484 1291

Swedish Franchise Association*, Box 5243, 402024 Goteborg, Sweden, Tel: 00 46 31 83 69 43, Fax: 00 46 31 81 10 72

Swiss Franchise Association*, Lowenstrasse 11 Postfach, 8023 Zurich, Switzerland, Tel: 00 41 1 225 47 57, Fax: 00 41 1 225 47 77

Turkish Franchise Association, Selime Hatun Camii Sokak, Ozlen Apt No 13/4, Gumussuyu, Istanbul, Turkey, Tel/fax: 00 99 1 252 5561

Yugoslav Franchise Association*, Mokranjeeva 28, 21000 Novi Sad, Yugoslavia, Tel/fax: 00 381 21 614 2321

* Members of the European Franchise Federation

APPENDIX B: BFA FULL MEMBERS

This list shows contact names, numbers and e-mail addresses, current in January 2000, together with the field of trading activity.

Alldays, Alldays House, Chestnut Avenue, Chandlers Ford, Southampton, SO53 3HJ, Mr M Robson, Tel: 01703 645000, E-mail: mrobson@alldays.co.uk *(Convenience stores)*

Alphagraphics, Thornburgh Road, Eastfield, Scarborough, YO11 3UY, Miss A Rogers, Tel: 01723 502222, E-mail: a.rogers@alphagraphics.co.uk *(Rapid response print, copy and publishing stores)*

Amtrak Express Parcels Ltd, Company House, Tower Hill, Bristol, BS2 0AZ, Mr M Jones, Tel: 01179 272002, E-mail: franchise.dept@amtrak.co.uk *(Overnight parcels collection & delivery)*

ANC, Parkhouse East Industrial Estate, Chesterton, Newcastle-under-Lyme, Staffordshire, ST5 7RB, Mr P Ronald, Tel: 01782 563322, Fax: 01782 563633, E-mail: franchise@anc.co.uk *(Express parcel delivery)*

Apollo Window Blinds Ltd, Cold Heseldon Industrial Estate, Seaham, County Durham, SR7 8ST, Mr G Mylchreest, Tel: 0191 513 0061, E-mail: hdwcjp@aol.com *(Manufacturers & retailers of window blinds to the domestic & commercial markets)*

Autela Components Ltd, Regal House, Birmingham Road, Stratford upon Avon, Warwickshire, CV37 OBN, Mr R Taylor, Tel: 01789 414273, E-mail: swhit@finelist.com *(Automotive part suppliers)*

Blazes Fireplace Centres Plc, Pendle House, Phoenix Way, Burnley, Lancs., BB11 5SX, Mr M Eyre, Tel: 01282 831176, E-mail: info@blazes.co.uk *(Fireplace & fire retailers offering a comprehensive service including installation)*

Budget Rent-a-Car International Inc., 41 Marlowes, Hemel Hempstead, Hertfordshire, HP1 1XJ, Ms Nikki Allen, Tel: 01442 276000, E-mail: nikki.allen@budget.co.uk *(National & international self-drive car, van & truck rental services)*

Card Connection, Park House, South Street, Farnham, Surrey, GU9 7QQ, Mr. Tony Winchester, Tel: 01252 892300, E-mail: ho@card-connection.co.uk *(Greeting card publisher, distributing through network of franchisees)*

Castle Estates, 178 Bridge Road, Sarisbury Green, Southampton, SO31 7EH, Mr Mike Edwards, Tel: 01489 - 573999, Fax: 01489 - 579816, E-mail: franchise@castle-estates.co.uk *(Residential property management)*

Chem Dry Northern & Southern (UK) Ltd, Colonial House, Swinemoor Lane, Beverley, East Riding of Yorkshire, HU17 0LS, Mr Steve Kilbey, Tel: 01482 872770, E-mail: info@chem-dry.co.uk

Chem Dry UK Midlands & London, Units 3&4 Mercian Park, Felspar Road, Amington Ind Estate, Tamworth, Staffs., B77 4DP, Mr Steve Kilbey, Tel: 01827 55644, E-mail: cmidlands@aol.com *(Carpet, upholstery & curtain cleaning service to domestic & commercial customers)*

Chemical Express, Spring Road, Smethwick, West Midlands, B66 1PT, Mr. L J Gray, Tel: 0121 525 4040, Fax: 0121 525 4919 *(Sell & distribute industrial hygiene, cleaning & maintenance chemicals via mobile showrooms)*

Clarks Shoes, 40 High Street, Street, Somerset, BA16 OYA, Mr R Marsden, Tel: 01458 443131, E-mail: roger.marsden@clarks.com *(Retail shoe shops)*

Colour Counsellors Ltd, 3 Dovedale Studios, 465 Battersea Park Road, London, SW11 4LR, Mrs V Stourton, Tel: 0171 978 5023, E-mail: headoffice@colourcounsellors.co.uk *(Interior decorating. Colour catalogued samples of wallpapers carpets & fabrics)*

Dairy Crest, Woburn House, 1 Duke Street, Luton, Beds., LU2 0HJ, Mr M Allen, Tel: 01582 681334, E-mail: markallen@dairycrest.co.uk *(Dairy products & food manufacturer)*

Dampcure Woodcure/30, Darley House, 41 Merton Road, Watford, Hertfordshire, WD1 7BU, Mrs C Darley, Tel: 01923 663322 *(Damp proofing & timber treatment)*

Delifrance, George Street House, George Street, Macclesfield, Cheshire, SK11 6HS, Mr Peter Hayes, Tel: 01625 610025, Fax: 01625 61259, E-mail: headoffice@slfgroup.demon.co.uk *(Traditional French bakery & café patisserie, retailing a variety of take away bakery products)*

Dominos Pizza, Lasborough Road, Kingston, Milton Keynes, MK10 0AB, Mr Anthony Round, Tel: 01908 580656, E-mail: anthonyr@dominos.co.uk *(Home delivery and takeaway pizza)*

Drain Doctor Ltd, Franchise House, Adam Court, Newark Road, Peterborough, Cambridgeshire, PE1 5PP, Mr F S Mitman, Tel: 01733 753939, E-mail: jan.mitman@virgin.net *(Plumbing)*

Driver Hire, Progress House, Castlefields Lane, Bingley, West Yorkshire, BD16 2AB, Mr A Cawthorn, Tel: 01274 551166, E-mail: info@driver-hire.co.uk *(Employment agency specialising in blue collar supply of temporary workers)*

Durham Pine, Colmia Avenue, Hylton Riverside, Sunderland, Tyne & Wear, SR5 3XF, Mrs Rita Ferguson, Tel: 0191 516 9300, E-mail: les@durhampine.com *(Specialist pine furniture retail outlets)*

Dyno Rod Developments Ltd, Zockoll House, 143 Maple Road, Surbiton, Surrey, KT6 4BJ, Mr J Chaplin, Tel: 0181 481 2200, E-mail: postmaster@dyno.com *(Property care franchises)*

Dyno-Rod Plc., Zockoll House, 143 Maple Road, Surbiton, Surrey, KY6 4BJ, Mr J Chaplin, Tel: 0181 481 2200, E-mail: postmaster@dyno.com *(Drain & pipe cleaning service)*

Express Dairies Ltd., Raines House, Denby Dale Road, Wakefield, WF1 1HR, Mr M Grey, Tel: 01924 290808, E-mail: mike-grey@express-dairies.co.uk *(The manufacture, processing, packaging, marketing & distribution of milk & dairy produce)*

Felicity Hat Hire, 2 Howick Park Avenue, Penwortham, Preston, PR1 0LS, Mr J Draper, Tel: 01772 742428, E-mail: franchise@felicity-uk.com *(Hiring of hats)*

Francesco Group, Woodings Yard, Bailey Street, Stafford, ST17 4BG, Mr F Dellicompagni, Tel: 01785 247175, E-mail: headoffice@francescogroup.co.uk *(Ladies & gentlemens hairdressing)*

Freedom Maintenance Ltd., Freedom House, Bradford Road, Tingley, Wakefield, WF3 1SD, Mr Steve Green, Tel: 01924 887766, E-mail: jtw@freedom-group.co.uk *(Building repair & maintenance)*

Green Flag, Green Flag House, Cote Lane, Leeds, LS28 5GF, Mr Graham Suddons, Tel: 0800 3288760, Fax: 0113 3904186, E-mail: franchisesales@greenflag.com *(Mobile vehicle inspection & servicing Vehicle Inspections, MOT Service Centres)*

Humana International Group plc., Humana House, 11 Eton High Street, Eton, Berkshire, SL4 6AT, Mr Kevin Cox, Tel: 01753 740020, E-mail: KCox@humana-intl.com *(Executive recruitment)*

In-Toto Ltd, Shaw Cross Court, Shaw Cross Business Park, Dewsbury, West Yorkshire, WF12 7RF, Mr D Watts, Tel: 01924 487900, E-mail: david.watts@intoto.co.uk *(Retailing of kitchens & bathroom furniture & appliances)*

Initial City Link, Wellington House, 61/73 Staines Road West, Sudbury on Thames, Middlesex, TW16 7AH, Mr Michael Cooke, Tel: 01932 822622, Fax: 01932 785560, E-mail: lindabrown@city-link.co.uk *(Same day & overnight parcel service)*

Inn Partnership Limited, Axis House, Tudor Road, Manor Park, Runcorn, WA7 1BD, Mr. M Grant, Tel: 0870 2412003, Fax: 01928 531005, E-mail: andy.cooke@innpartnership.co.uk *(Public House retailing)*

Interlink Express Parcels Ltd, Brunswick Court, Brunswick Square, Bristol, BS2 8PE, Mr K Gillard, Tel: 0117 944 0000, E-mail: jroy@interlinkexpress.co.uk *(Overnight parcels collection & delivery)*

Kall-Kwik Printing (UK) Ltd., Kall-Kwik House, 106 Pembroke Road, Ruislip, Middlesex, HA4 8NW, Ms J Twining, Tel: 01895 872000, E-mail: franchise-sales@kallkwik.co.uk *(Quick printing centre offering comprehensive design printing finishing photocopying service)*

Legal & General Estate Agency, 68 School Road, Tilehurst, Reading, Berks., RG31 5AW, Mr Michael Stoop, Tel: 0118 9429470, Fax: 0118 9452768, E-mail: admin@lgfl.co.uk *(Estate Agency)*

Master Thatchers Ltd., Fircross Offices, Stratfield Saye, Reading, Berkshire, RG7 2BT, Mr R C West, Tel: 01256 880828 *(Thatching in water reed & combed wheat reed including repairs patching & re-ridging)*

McDonald's, 11-59 High Road, East Finchley, London, N2 8AW, Miss Krissy Elliott, Tel: 0181 700 7153, Fax: 0181 700 7469, E-mail: kelliott@uk.mcd.com *(Quick service food restaurant)*

Mercury Express UK Ltd., 53/54 Hamilton Square, Birkenhead, Wirral, L41 5AS, Mr R Glynn, Tel: 0151 6661852, E-mail: rglynn1@compuserve.com *(Same day light haulage)*

Metro-Rod, Metro House, Churchill Way, Macclesfield, Cheshire, SK11 6AY, Mr Charles Sindall, Tel: 01625 434444, E-mail: wendy.ayres@thameswater.co.uk *(Drain care and repair for the domestic, commercial and industrial markets)*

Minster Services Group UK, Minster House, 948-952 Kingsbury Road, Erdington, Birmingham, B24 9PZ, Mr Alan Haigh, Tel: 0121 386 1186, E-mail: birmingham@minstergroup.co.uk *(Management of contract office cleaning services)*

Molly Maid UK, Vale House, 100 Vale Road, Windsor, Berkshire, SL4 5JL, Mrs P Bader, Tel: 01753 829400, E-mail: Mollymaiduk.com@btinternet.com *(Domestic cleaning services)*

Mr Clutch, 2 Priory Road, Strood, Rochester, Kent, ME2 2EG, Mr Joe Yussuf, Tel: 01634 717747 *(Fast fit of clutches, gearboxes, brakes)*

Nationwide Investigations Group Limited, Newland House, 3 Hazel Grove Road, Haywards Heath, West Sussex, RH16 3PH, Mr A Hipperson, Tel: 01444 416004, E-mail: franchise@nig.co.uk *(Private investigations bureau)*

Neal's Yard Remedies, 26-34 Ingate Place, Battersea, London, SW8 3NS, Ms R Fraser, Tel: 0171 4981686, E-mail: mail@nealsyardremedies.com

PDC International Limited, 1 Church Lane, East Grinstead, West Sussex, RH19 3AZ, Mr Stephen Ricketts, Tel: 01342 315321, E-mail: pdc@pdc-intl.demon.co.uk *(Quick printing shops)*

Perfect Pizza, Units 5 & 6 The Forum, Hanworth Lane, Chertsey, Surrey, KT16 9JX, Mr M Clayton, Tel: 01932 568000, E-mail: martin_clayton @perfectpizza.co.uk *(Fast food take-aways and deliveries)*

Pirtek Europe plc., 35 Acton Park Estate, The Vale, Acton, London, W3 7QE, Mr P Brennan, Tel: 0181 749 8444, E-mail: joanne@pirtekuk.com *(Hydraulic & industrial hoses & assemblies from depots & mobiles)*

Pitman Training Group, Pitman House, Audby Lane, Wetherby, West Yorkshire, LS22 7FD, Mr J O'Brien, Tel: 01937 548500, E-mail: Pitman.FSA@pitman-training.co.uk *(Careers, IT and Office Skills Training Centres)*

Post Office Counters Ltd, Franchise Project Manager, Gavrelle House, 2-14 Bunhill Row, London, EC1Y 8HQ, Mr Chris Sutton, Tel: 0171 776 3545, E-mail: lesley.cartwright@postoffice.co.uk *(Retail & Post Office Products)*

Practical Car & Van Rental, 21/23 Little Broom Street, Camp Hill, Birmingham, B12 0EU, Mr. B Agnew, Tel: 0121 772 8599, E-mail: rental@practical.co.uk *(Vehicle rental)*

Prontaprint Ltd, Axis 6, Rhodes Way, North Watford Industrial Estate, Watford, WD2 4YW, Ms Heather Prescott, Tel: 01923 691400, Fax: 01923 229211, E-mail: heather.prescott@prontaprint.com *(Fast print centres incorporating artwork & design commercial copying & business communications services)*

Rainbow International Carpet Care and Restoration Specialist, Spectrum House, Lower Oakham Way, Oakham Business Park, Mansfield, NG18 5BY, Mr R Hutton, Tel: 01623 422488, E-mail: ron@rainbow-int.co.uk *(Supply of maintenance services for soft furnishings and disaster restoration)*

Recognition Express Ltd, PO Box 7, 7 Rugby Road, Hinckley, Leicestershire, LE10 2NE, Mr T A Howorth, Tel: 01455 232236, E-mail: terry@recognition-express.com *(Manufacture & sale of personalised name badges, interior & exterior signage, vehicle livery, trophies & awards)*

Ribbon Revival, Caslon Court, Pitronnerie Road, St Peter Port, Guernsey, GY1 2RW, Mr M Williams, Tel: 01481 729552, E-mail: ribbonrevival@ribbonrevival.net *(Manufacturers & suppliers of office products)*

Safeclean International, 152 Milton Park, Abingdon, Oxon, OX14 4SD, Mr Stan Knight, Tel: 01235 444700, E-mail: safeclean@lillyuk.com *(Professional furniture care & expert spot stain removal)*

Saks Hair (Holdings) Ltd/Command Performance, 2 Peel Court, St Cuthberts Way, Darlington, Co Durham, DL1 1GB, Mr D Cheesebrough, Tel: 01325 380333, E-mail: sakshq@compuserve.com *(Ladies & gentlemens hairdressing)*

Securicor Omega Express-Sameday, Comewell House, North Street, Horsham, West Sussex, BN12 1BQ, Mrs D Shaddick, Tel: 01403 264164, E-mail: fliz.patterson@sms.securicor.co.uk *(Sameday & overnight express parcels courier)*

Select Appointments plc., Regent Court, Laporte Way, Beds., LU4 8SB, Mr T Mundella, Tel: 01582 811600, Fax: 01582 811611, E-mail: franchise@select.co.uk *(Recruitment consultancy)*

ServiceMaster Ltd., ServiceMaster House, Leicester Road, Anstey, Leicester, LE7 7AT, Mr D Rudge, Tel: 0116 2364646, E-mail: servicemaster@servicemaster.demon.co.uk *(Professional cleaning services for commercial domestic& insurance customers. Furnishing and carpet repairs & restoration)*

Signs Express, The Old Church, St Matthews Road, Norwich, NR1 1SP, Mr D Corbett, Tel: 01603 625925, E-mail: fran@signsexpress.co.uk *(Sign makers)*

Snap-on-Tools, Telford Way, Kettering, Northants, NN16 8SN, Mr T Barcham, Tel: 01536 413800, Fax: 01536 413900, E-mail: ukweb@snapon.com *(Automotive tool products)*

Snappy Snaps Franchises Ltd, Glenthorne Mews, Glenthorne Road, Hammersmith, London, W6 OLJ, Mr T MacAndrews, Tel: 0181 741 7474, E-mail: info@snappysnaps.co.uk *(One hour developing & printing of films photographic services & associated products)*

Spud U Like Ltd., 9 Central Business Centre, Great Central Way, London, NW10 0UR, Mr T Schleisinger, Tel: 0181 830 2424, E-mail: headoffice@spudulike.com *(Fast food restaurants based on baked potatoes with large variety of fillings)*

The Body Shop, Watersmead, Littlehampton, West Sussex, BN17 6LS, Mr Nick Benbow, Tel: 01903 731500, Fax: 01903 844383, E-mail: info@bodyshop.co.uk *(Cosmetic & toiletry retailer)*

The Flat Roof Company, Unit 7 Guardian Park, Station Industrial Estate, Tadcaster, N Yorks, LS24 9SG, Mr Kevin Moody, Tel: 01937 530788, E-mail: enquiries@flatroof.co.uk *(Refurbishment of flat roofs using a bonded resin system)*

Thorntons, Thornton Park, Somercotes, Derby, DE55 4XJ, Ms Colette Suddes, Tel: 01773 540550, E-mail: franchise@thorntons.co.uk *(Specialist chocolate & sugar confectionery)*

Thrifty Car Rental, The Old Courthouse, Hughendon Road, High Wycombe, Bucks, HP13 5DT, Mr Graham Bullock, Tel: 01494 751500, Fax: 01494 751503, E-mail: marketing@thrifty.co.uk *(Car & Van Rental)*

Toni & Guy, Innovia House, Central Way, North Feltham Trading Estate, Feltham, TW14 0QZ, Mr John Murphy, Tel: 0181 844 0008, E-mail: clarissa@mascolo.co.uk *(Hairdressing)*

Travail Employment Group Ltd, 4 Southgate Street, Gloucester, GL1 2DP, Ms P Zwar, Tel: 01452 420700, E-mail: franchise@travail.co.uk *(Business employment agency)*

Unigate Dairies Ltd., 14/40 Victoria Road, Aldershot, Hampshire, GU1 1TH, Mr H Allam, Tel: 01252 366966 *(Distribution of milk & dairy products & soft drinks)*

Vendo plc., 215 East Lane, Wembley, Middlesex, HA0 3NG, Mr I Calhoun, Tel: 0181 908 1234 *(Commercial vehicle power washing)*

Vision Express, Abbeyfield Road, Lenton, Nottingham, NG7 2SP, Mr Peter Watson, Tel: 01159 882013, Fax: 01159 882380, E-mail: joanne.redfern@visionexpress.com *(Retail opticians)*

Whitegates Ltd., 7 Lower Ouse Gate, York, North Yorks, YO1 1QX, Mr Roger Ellison, Tel: 01904 626463, Fax: 01904 626473, E-mail: ellison@whitegates92.fsnet.co.uk *(Residential estate agency)*

Wimpy International Ltd., 2 The Listons, Liston Road, Marlow, Buckinghamshire, SL7 1FD, Mr Brian Crambac, Tel: 01628 891655, E-mail: mailroom@wimpy-restaurants.com *(Family hamburger restaurant)*

APPENDIX C: BFA ASSOCIATES

This list shows contact names, numbers and e-mail addresses, current in January 2000, together with the field of trading activity.

021 Courier Services Limited, Unit 4, Bannerley Road, Garretts Green, Birmingham, B33 0SL, Mr Paul Fox, Tel: 0121 789 9922, E-mail: sales@021couriers.com *(Same day courier services)*

Advanced Hair Studios, 46 Fitzray Street, London, W1P 5HS, Mr Carl Howell, Tel: 0171 3834591, Fax: 0171 3880615, E-mail: carlhowell@advancedhairstudio.com *(Hair replacement programmes)*

Auditel, St Paul's Gate, Cross Street, Winchester, Hants., SO23 8SZ, Mr C Allison, Tel: 01962 863915, E-mail: info@auditel.net *(Cost management consultants in areas of communications, energy & facilities management)*

Bang & Olufsen, 630 Wharfedale Road, Winnersh Triangle, Wokingham, Berks., RG41 5TP, Mr D Mottershead, Tel: 0118 969 2288, E-mail: cgr@bang-olufsen.dk *(Retail television & hi-fi)*

Barrett & Coe, 79A Thorpe Road, Norwich, Norfolk, NR1 1UA, Mr. Andrew Coe, Tel: 01603 629739, E-mail: enquire@barrett&coe.co.uk *(Photographic services)*

Café Nescafe, Beverages Division, St George's House, Croydon, Surrey, CR9 1NR, Mrs L Robinson, Tel: 0181 667 5536, E-mail: louise.robinson@nestlegb.nestle.com *(Branded retail coffee shops)*

Card Line Greetings Ltd, Units 4-5 Hale Trading Estate, Lower Church Lane, Tipton, West Midlands, DY4 7PQ , Mr. M Crapper, Tel: 0121 522 4407, E-mail: info@cardline.co.uk *(Distribution of greetings cards)*

Cash Generator, 113 Bradshawgate, Bolton, Lancs., BL1 1QD, Mr BC Lewis, Tel: 01204 37187, E-mail: info@cashgenerator.co.uk *(Retailer of pre-used items, pawnbrokers and cheque changers)*

Cheque Convertors, 11-13 Limes Court, Conduit Lane, Hoddesdon, Herts., EN11 8EP, Mr K Roberts, Tel: 01992 478991, E-mail: sales@bccgroup.u-net.com *(Cheque cashing)*

Choices Video, The Home Entertainment Corporation plc., 19-24 Manesty Road, Orton Southgate, Peterborough, PE2 6UP, Mr J M Sealey, Tel: 01733 231231 *(Video hire & sale)*

CNA Executive Search, Garden Court, Lockington Hall, Lockington, Derby, DE74 2RH, Ms Paula Reed, Tel: 01509 670022, E-mail: cna.international@btinternet.com *(Executive Recruitment)*

Colneis Marketing, York House, 2/4 York Road, Felixstowe, Suffolk, IP11 7QQ, Mr J Botting, Tel: 01394 27166, E-mail: john@colneis.f9.co.uk *(Greeting cards)*

Drinkmaster Ltd., Plymouth Road, Liskeard, Cornwall, PL14 3PG, Ms M Bunton, Tel: 01579 342082, E-mail: mbunton@drinkmaster.co.uk *(Manufacturer & distributor of flavour sealed beverage capsules & dispensing equipment)*

Dublcheck, Padeswood Hall, Padeswood, Mold, Flintshire, CH7 4JF, Mr Chris Davies, Tel: 01244 550150, E-mail: dublcheck @mail.dublcheck.co.uk *(Commercial Cleaning Services)*

Eismann International Ltd., Margarethe House, Eismann Way, Phoenix Park Ind Estate, Corby, NN17 1ZB, Mr J Wilfling, Tel: 01536 275100, Fax: 01538 275106, E-mail: cmgivern@eismann.co.uk *(Home delivery of frozen foods)*

Expense Reduction Analysts Ltd., St Paul's Gate, Cross Street, Winchester, Hants, SO23 8SZ, Mr R Allison, Tel: 01962 849444, E-mail: r.allison@expense-reduction.net *(Cost consultants)*

Fastrack Parcels Limited, Fastrack House, Harrington Way, Bermuda Industrial Estate, Bermuda Park, Nuneaton, CV10 7FT, Mr Ken Rostron, Tel: 01203 345511, E-mail: it@fastrack.co.uk *(Next day delivery - documents, parcels, freight)*

Fastsigns, 36 High Street, New Malden, Surrey, KT3 4HE, Ms S Kailey, Tel: 0181 336 0802, E-mail: peter.bennison@fastsigns.com *(Fast service, fully computerised. high profile sign shops)*

Fix A Chip, The Car Smart Centre, Vermont, Washington, Tyne & Wear, NE37 2AX, Mr Steve Harrison, Tel: 0191 417 0577 *(Job format mobile minor vehicle repairs)*

Formative Fun Ltd., The Old School, Gundry Lane, Bridport, Dorset, DT6 6RL, Mrs Jane Warren, Tel: 01297 489880, E-mail: jane@formative-fun.com *(The marketing of educational toys, games & books in an advisory capacity)*

Fresh Connection, 166 Bute Street Mall, Arndale Centre, Luton, LU1 2TL, Ms Pauline Marsden, Tel: 01582 422781 *(Retail fresh bakery & takeaway foods)*

Garage Door Associates Ltd., Unit 5 Meadow Broo, Industrial Centre, Maxwell Way, Crawley, West Sussex, RH10 2SA, Mr D Hibbart, Tel: 01293 611598, E-mail: gda-franchise@gd-hq.demon.co.uk *(Retail sale and installation of garage doors, electric garage door operators, gates and gate openers, ancillary equipment)*

Green Thumb, Basingwerk Suite, Greenfield Business Centre, Greenfield, Holywell, Flintshire, CH8 7QB, Mr Stephen Waring,   Tel: 01325 718062, Fax: 01325 718063, E-mail: franchise@greenthumb.co.uk *(Domestic lawn treatment service)*

Harry Ramsden's, Larwood House, Whitecross, Guiseley, LS20 8LZ, Mr R Richardson, Tel: 01943 879531, E-mail: richardr@harryramsdens.co.uk *(Fish & chip restaurant and take-away)*

Helen O`Grady's Childrens Drama Academy, Gerenne House, Rue de la Cache, St Sampsons, Guernsey, GY2 4AF, Mr N Le Page, Tel: 01481 54419, E-mail: hogrady@compuserve.com *(Operation of academies offering a self development programme for children, using a unique drama syllabus)*

Jani-King, 150 London Road, Kingston upon Thames, Surrey, KT2 6QL, Mr P Howorth, Tel: 0181 481 4300, Fax: 0181 481 4343   *(Contract cleaning)*

Leading Agencies, 4 Hewell Lane, Tardebigge, Bromsgrove, Worcs., B60 1LP, Mr T Conry, Tel: 07000 717273, E-mail: info@leadingagencies.co.uk *(High quality residential letting and management)*

Likisma, Dolphin House, Dennington Road, Wellingborough, Northants., NN29 7NN, Ms Lisa Burke, Tel: 01933 440727, Fax: 01933 440733, E-mail: enquiries@likisma.co.uk *(Direct sales company marketing a range of aromatherapy and natural bodycare products)*

Martin & Co., 6-8 Union Street, Yeovil, Somerset, BA20 1PQ, Mr T Rose, Tel: 01935 426000, E-mail: mail@houserentals.demon.co.uk *(Property Management and Lettings)*

Master Brew, Beverages House, 7 Ember Court, Hersham Trading Estate, Hersham, KT12 3PT, Mr F Vanvilborg, Tel: 01932 253787, E-mail: info@miko.co.uk *(Supplying ground coffees & a complete beverage range to offices & caterers)*

Metal Supermarkets, Unit B Colliery Lane, Banton Road, Exhall, Coventry, CV7 9EJ, Mr Alan Tilley, Tel: 01203 366301, Fax: 01203 366149, E-mail: 113413.3436@compuserve.com *(Retailers of ready cut metals)*

Nippers, Mansers, Nizels Lane, Hildenborough, Kent, TN11 8NX, Mrs J Cassel, Tel: 01732 838333, E-mail: nippers@which.net *(Retail nursery goods & toys)*

O'Briens Irish Sandwich Bars, 24 South Williams Street, Dublin 2, Ireland, Ms Olive Hipwell, Tel: 00353 16715176, Fax: 00353 16708918, E-mail: info@obriens.ie *(Sandwich Café)*

Oscar Pet Foods, Bannister Hall Mill, Higher Walton, Preston, Lancashire, PR5 4DB, Mr M Dancy, Tel: 01772 626789, E-mail: discover@oscars.co.uk *(Pet Food Home Delivery)*

Prestige Nursing, 18 Barnmead, Haywoods Heath, W Sussex, RH16 1UZ, Ms Linda Hutson, Tel: 0181 2888830, Fax: 0181 2888839, E-mail: j.bruce@prestige-nursing.co.uk *(Health Care Recruitment)*

Re-Nu, 60 Nuffield Road, Nuffield Industrial Estate, Poole, Dorset, BH17 0RS, Ms Meryl Ponsford, Tel: 01202 687642 *(Replacement kitchen & bedrooms made to measure doors & allied accessories)*

Rosemary Conley Diet & Fitness Clubs Ltd., Quorn House, Meeting Street, Quorn, Loughborough, Leicestershire, LE12 8EX, Mr Simon Ford, General Manager, Tel: 01509 620222, E-mail: Maxine.Baxter@rosemary-conley.co.uk *(Diet & fitness clubs)*

Sevenoaks Hi-Fi & Video, 109-113 London Road, Sevenoaks, Kent, TN13 1BH, Mr M Blockley, Tel: 01494 431290, E-mail: sevenoaksoundvis@aol.com *(Electrical Retail)*

Signs Now, 478 Stafford Road, Oxley, Wolverhampton, WV10 6AN, Mr B Dunphy, Tel: 01902 398999, E-mail: bill@270.signsnow.co.uk *(Design, manufacture and installation of signs)*

Sinclair Collis, Lower Walsall Street, Wolverhampton, West Midlands, WV1 2ES, Mr J Banks, Tel: 01902 352515 *(The supply of tobacco products vending machines)*

Snack in the Box, Dunbeath Lodge, 3 Eastern Road, Havant, Hants, PO9 2JE, Mr J Lynham, Tel: 01705 799023, E-mail: info@snackinthebox.freeserve.co.uk *(Snack delivery to businesses)*

Sportsmania, Acorn Way, Oaktree Business Park, Mansfield, NG18 3HD, Mr David Hoskins, Tel: 01623 428197, Fax: 01623 428198, E-mail: davidhoskins@sportsmania.co.uk *(Wholesaling of branded and unbranded sportswear. All products are heavily discounted.)*

Stagecoach Theatre Arts, The Courthouse, Elm Grove, Walton on Thames, Surrey, KT12 1LH, Ms A Cawdron, Tel: 01932 254333, E-mail: stagecoach@dial.pipex.com *(Part-time theatre schools for children aged 6-16)*

Stainbusters Ltd, 15 Windmill Avenue, Woolpit Business Park, Woolpit, Bury St Edmunds, Suffolk, IP30 9UP, Ms E Edwards, Tel: 01359 243800, E-mail: tom.edwards@stainbustersint.com *(Carpet & upholstery cleaning)*

Status Hydraulics, Status House, Cambrian Business Park, Queens Lane, Mold, Flintshire, CH7 1XB, Mr J Harris, Tel: 01352 707800, E-mail: status@status-hydraulics.com *(Hydraulic hose fittings and allied services supplied via mobile service units and trade counters)*

Stumpbusters UK Ltd, PO Box 1064, Maidenhead, Berks, SL6 6AS, Mr A Broom, Tel: 01628 484547, Fax: 01628 488757, E-mail: stump@globalnet.co.uk *(Tree stump grinding specialists)*

TaxAssist Direct Limited, TaxAssist House, 58 Thorpe Road, Norwich, NR1 1RY, Mrs L. Charleton, Tel: 01603 611811, Fax: 01603 619992, E-mail: email@taxassist.co.uk *(Accounting services)*

The Wheelie Bin Cleaning Co., The Channel Business Centre, 11 Bouverie Square, Folkestone, Kent, CT20 1BD, Mr Kevyn Lloyd, Tel: 01303 850856, Fax: 01303 221099, E-mail: sales@wheeliebin.com *(Cleaning wheelie bins)*

Uniglobe, Parkside, 4 Calverley Park Gardens, Tunbridge Wells, Kent, TN1 2JN, Mr M Levy, Tel: 01892 507800, Fax: 01892 507801, E-mail: mlevy@uniglobetravel.co.uk *(Business & leisure travel agencies)*

Urban Planters, 202 Pasture Lane, Bradford, West Yorkshire, BD7 2SE, Mr N Gresty, Tel: 01274 579331, E-mail: may@urbanplanters.co.uk *(Supply (on sale & rental) of indoor plants, with maintenance service)*

Ventrolla Ltd., 11 Hornbeam Square South, South Harrogate, North Yorkshire, HG2 8NB, Mr S C Emmerson, Tel: 01423 870011, E-mail: franchise@ventrolla.co.uk *(Renovating and performance upgrading of existing windows using patented system)*

VIP Bin Cleaning, The Coach House, Commercial Road, Dereham, Norfolk, NR19 1AE, Mr M Harvey, Tel: 01362 851185, E-mail: enquiries@vipbincleaning.co.uk *(Bin cleaning)*

Worldwide Refinishing Systems, Spectrum House, Lower Oakham Way, Oakham Business Park, Mansfield, NG18 5BY, Mr M Lusty, Tel: 01623 422439, E-mail: phil@rainbow-int.co.uk *(Bathroom & kitchen refinishing & remodelling)*

APPENDIX D: BFA AFFILIATES

This list shows contact names, numbers and e-mail addresses, current in January 2000, together with websites where known.

BANKS

Barclays Bank plc., Franchise Department, Avon House, PO Box 120 Longwood Close, Westwood Business Park, Coventry, CV4 8JN, Mrs H Dullehan, Tel: 02476 534474, Fax: 01203 532749, E-Mail: bev.willacy@barclays.co.uk Web site: www.barclays.co.uk/business.html

HSBC, Franchise Unit, 10 Lower Thames Street, London, EC3R 6AE, Mrs C Hayes, Tel: 0171 260 6783, E-Mail: miriaim.fox@hsbc.group.com Web site: www.banking.hsbc.co.uk

Lloyds TSB, Business Banking, UKRB, PO Box 112, Canon's Way, Bristol, BS99 7LB, Mr. S McLauchlan, Tel: 0117 943 3089, E-Mail: sally.kowalski@lloydstsb.co.uk, Web site: www.lloydsbank.co.uk/franchis/

NatWest UK, Retail Banking Services - Franchise Section, Level 10 Drapers Gardens, 12 Throgmorton Avenue, London, EC2N 2DL,   Mr. D Costello, Tel: 0171 920 5966 Web site: www.natwest.co.uk

The Royal Bank of Scotland plc., Franchise and Licensing Department, PO Box 31, 42 St Andrew Street, Edinburgh, EH2 2YE, Mr. G Rose, Tel: 0131 556 1818, Fax: 0131 523 2178, E-Mail: smitdgb@rbos.co.uk Web site: www.rbs.co.uk/franchise/

BUSINESS SOFTWARE PROVIDERS

Thomson Directories, 296 Farnborough Road, Farnborough, Hants., GU14 7NU, Ms D Hage, Tel: 01252 390449, Fax: 01252 390402, E-Mail: sue.maguire@thomweb.co.uk

CHARTERED ACCOUNTANTS

Beresfords, Castle House, Castle Hill Avenue, Folkestone, Kent, CT20 2TQ, Mr T C Hindle, Tel: 01303 850992, Fax: 01303 850979, E-Mail: beresfords@folkestone1.demon.co.uk

Fraser Russell, Crown House, Gloucester Road, Redhill, Surrey, RH1 1AZ , Mr R J Mitchell, Tel: 01737 854100, Fax: 01737 760407, E-Mail: fraser-russell.redhill@dial.pipex.com

Levy Gee, 66 Wigmore Street, London, W1H 0HQ, Mr J Synett,   Tel: 0171 467 4000, E-Mail: info@levygee.co.uk Web site: www.levygee.co.uk

Rees Pollock, 7 Pilgrim Street, London, EC4V 6DR, Mr W A Pollock Tel: 0171 329 6404, E-Mail: andy@reespollock.co.uk Web site: www.reespollock.co.uk

Watson Dunne & Co, Oakfield House, 378 Brandon Street, Motherwell, ML1 1XA, Mr Terry Dunne, Tel: 01698 250251, Fax: 01698 250261, E-Mail: WatsonDunn@aol.com

DEVELOPMENT AGENCIES

Forth Valley Enterprise, Laurel House, Laurelhill Business Park, Stirling, FK7 9JQ, Mr Bill Cook, Tel: 01786 451919, Fax: 01786 452222, E-Mail: fvinfo@scotent.co.uk

Scottish Enterprise, 120 Bothwell Street, Glasgow, G2 7JP, Dr. B McVey, Tel: 0141 248 2700, E-Mail: brain.mcvey@scotent.co.uk

EXHIBITION ORGANISERS

CDFEX, 78 Carlton Place, Glasgow, G5 9TH, Mr J Sellyn, Tel: 0141 429 5900, E-Mail: sellynj@cdfex.com

Miller Freeman UK Limited, 630 Chiswick High Road, London, W4 5BG, Mr C Gillam, Tel: 0181 742 2828, E-Mail: CGillam@unmf.co.uk

Venture Marketing Group Ltd. Carlton Plaza, 111 Upper Richmond Road, Putney, London, SW15 2TJ, Mr. D Tuck, Tel: 0181 785 2288, E-Mail: alison.marshall@vmgl.com

FACTORS

Griffin Credit Services Ltd., Griffin House, 21 Farncombe Road, Worthing, West Sussex, BN11 2BW, Mr B J Cooper, Tel: 01903 205181, Fax: 01903 214101, E-Mail: gcs@dial.pipex.com

FRANCHISE CONSULTANTS

AW Franchising & Marketing, Whalley Banks Farm, Dean Lane, Whalley, Lancashire, BB7 9JL, Mr Andrew Whitaker, Tel: 01254 824549

BDO Stoy Hayward Management Consultants, 8 Baker Street, London, W1M 1DA, Mr. Max Mc Hardy, Tel: 0171 486 5888, E-Mail: max.mchardy@bdo.co.uk   Web site: www.bdo.co.uk

CFM Consulting, The Old Manse, Lunghurst Road, Woldingham, Surrey, CR3 7HF, Mr D Taube, Tel: 01883 653178, E-Mail: dtaube@cfmconsulting.demon.co.uk www.cfmconsulting.demon.co.uk

Equitas Group, The Grange Management Centre, Heyford Lane, Stowe Hill, Northants, NN7 4SF, Mr P Loryman, Tel: 01327 340408, Fax: 01327 349242

Franchise & Marketing Management Ltd (FMM), 46/48 Thornhill Road, Streetly, Sutton Coldfield, West Midlands, B74 3EH, Mr. Mike Matthews, Tel: 0121 353 0031/2, E-Mail: consult@fmm1mid.demon.co.uk Web site: www.fmmconsult.co.uk

Franchise Development Services - Providing national and international franchise consultancy services. Publishers of The Franchise Magazine, Franchise International & The United Kingdom Directory, Franchise House, 56 Surrey Street, Norwich, NR1 3FD, E-Mail: fds@norwich.com

Franchise Development Services (London) - Providing national & international franchise consultancy services. Publishers of The Franchise Magazine, Franchise International & The United Kingdom Directory, 10 Greenaway Gardens, London, NW3 7DJ, Mr. L H Levi, Tel: 0171 794 6356, E-Mail: franlondon@aol.com

Franchise Development Services (Southern) - Providing national & international franchise consultancy services. Publishers of The Franchise Magazine, Franchise International & The United Kingdom Directory, Maple Grove, Bradfield, Reading, Berks, RG7 6DH, Mr. Gordon Patterson, Tel: 01189 745115, E-Mail: fdss.patterson@ukonline.co.uk

Franchise Directions, Status 4, Status Park, Bath Road, Hayes, Middlesex, UB3 5EY, Mr. S Brown, Tel: 0181 754 9695, Fax: 0181 754 9273, E-Mail: retail.directions@online.rednet.co.uk

Horwath Franchising, 25 New Steet Square, London, EC4A 3LN, Mr. Brian Duckett, Tel: 0171 917 9824, E-Mail: duckettb@horwathcw.co.uk Web site: www.horwath.com

Nina Moran Watson, Franchise Consultants, The Lodge House, Crow Lane, Tendring, Essex, CO16 9AP, Ms. Nina Moran Watson, Tel: 01255 830045, mobile 07968 445804, E-Mail: nmoran-watson@btclick.com, home.btclick.com/nmoran-watson

Nina Moran Watson, Franchise Consultants, 74 Kirk Street, Strathaven, ML10 6BA, Mr Euan Fraser, Tel: 01357 523308, E-Mail: efraser@ibm.net

Opta Enterprises (CI) Limited - National and International Franchise Development services specialising in the US Franchise Market. Barclay Chambers, Grande Rue, St Martins, Guernsey, GY4 6LH

Mr J Scott, Tel: 01481 233255, E-Mail: johns.opta@guernsey.net Web site: www.opta.guernsey.net

Peter Williams, 40 Newquay Close, Nuneaton, Warwickshire, CV11 6FH, Mr. P Williams, Tel: 01203 329260

TDA - Enterprising Futures, 4 Thameside Centre, Kew Bridge Road, Brentford, Middx, TW8 9HF, Mr P Tough, Tel: 0181 568 3040, Fax: 0181 569 9800, E-Mail: vmdunn@tdaconsulting.co.uk

The Franchise Company, Ashburn House, 84 Grange Road, Darlington, Co Durham, DL1 5NP, Miss. J Waites, Tel: 01325 251455, Fax: 01325 251466, E-Mail: frank@franchisecompany.co.uk Web site: www.franchisecompany.co.uk

FRANCHISE MANUAL PUBLISHING CONSULTANTS

Manual Writers International, 49 Bradmore Park Road, London, W6 0DT, Mrs P Hopkinson, Tel: 07000 315750, E-Mail: manual_writers@compuserve.com   Web site: www.british-franchise.org.uk/manual_writers/

INSURANCE BROKERS

NatWest Insurance Services Ltd. PO Box 106, 37 Broad Street, Bristol, BS99 7NQ, Mr Richard Saunders, Tel: 0117 92633676, E-Mail: richard.saunders@nwis.co.uk

Pentagon Insurance Brokers, Polygon Hall, PO Box 225, Le Marchant Street, St Peter Port, Guernsey, GY1 4HY, Mr K Bradley, Tel: 01481 728002, E-Mail: kbradley@polygon.co.uk

Tolsen, 148 King Street, London, W6 0QU, Mr D Perfect, Tel: 0181 741 8361, E-Mail: vwheatcroft@tolsonmessenger.co.uk

RECRUITMENT CONSULTANTS

CNA Executive Search (Kensington), Queens Chambers, King Street, Nottingham, NG1 2BH, Ms L Stojko, Tel: 0115 958 9985

SOLICITORS

Addleshaw Booth & Co., Dennis House, Marsden Street, Manchester, M2 1JD, Mr G Lindrup, Tel: 0161 832 5994, Fax: 0181 9609655, E-Mail: jwd@addleshaw-booth.co.uk

Biggart Baillie & Gifford, Dalmore House, 310 St Vincent Street, Glasgow, G2 5QR, Mr C Miller, Tel: 0141 228 8000, E-Mail: info@biggartbaillie.co.uk

Brodies, 15 Atholl Crescent, Edinburgh, EH3 8HA, Mr JCA Voge, Tel: 0131 228 3777, E-Mail: mailbox@brodies.co.uk

Burstows, 8 Ifield Road, Crawley, West Sussex, RH11 7YY, Mrs C Armitage, Tel: 01293 603603, Fax: 01293 603666, E-Mail: caroline.armitage@asb-law.com

Chambers & Co, Jonathan Scott Hall, Thorpe Road, Norwich, NR1 1UH, Mr J Chambers, Tel: 01603 616155, E-Mail: chambers@paston.co.uk

Clairmonts, 9 Clairmont Gardens, Glasgow, G3 7LW, Mr DS Kaye, Tel: 0141 3314000, E-Mail: info@clairmonts.co.uk

David Bigmore & Co., 36 Whitefriars Street, London, EC4Y 8BH, Mr. D Bigmore, BFA Legal Committee, Tel: 0171 583 2277

Eversheds, Sun Alliance House, 35 Mosley Street, Newcastle Upon Tyne, NE1 1XX, Mr. P Heatherington, Tel: 0191 2611661 ext 5312, Fax: 0191 2618267, E-Mail: paulhetherington@eversheds.co.uk

Eversheds, Cloth Hall Court, Infirmary Street, Leeds, LS1 2JB, Mr P Heatherington, Tel: 0113 2430391, E-Mail: paulhetherington@eversheds.co.uk

Eversheds, 1 Royal Standard Place, Nottingham, NG1 6FZ, Mr M Knibbs, Tel: 0115 950 7000, E-Mail: nottingham@eversheds.com

Eversheds, Fitzalan House, Fitzalan Road, Cardiff, CF2 1XZ, Mrs H McNabb, Tel: 01222 471147, E-Mail: Heathermcnabb@eversheds.com

Eversheds, 10 Newhall Street, Birmingham, B3 3LX, Mr P Manford, Tel: 0121 233 2001, E-Mail: petermanford@eversheds.co.uk

Eversheds, Senator House, 85 Queen Victoria Street, London, EC4V 4JL, Mr M Mendelsohn, BFA Legal Committee, Tel: 0171 919 4500, E-Mail: mendelm@eversheds.com

Eversheds, 11-12 Queen Squarel, Bristol, BS1 4NT, Mr P Sampson, Tel: 0117 929 555, E-Mail: paulsampson@eversheds.com

Field Fisher Waterhouse, 41 Vine Street, London, EC3N 2AA, Mr M Abell, BFA Legal Committee, Tel: 0171 481 4841, E-Mail: pma@ffwlaw.com

Hammond Suddards, 16 John Dalton Street, Manchester, M60 8HS, Mrs P Cowie, Tel: 0161 8305000, E-Mail: Pauline.Cowie@HammondSuddards.co.uk

Hammond Suddards, 7 Devonshire Gardens, London, EC2M 4YH, E-Mail: Mrs P Cowie, Tel: 0171 6551000, Pauline.Cowie@HammondSuddards.co.uk

JST Mackintosh, Colonial Chambers, Temple Street, Liverpool, L2 5RH, Mr G Howard Jones, Tel: 0151 282 2828, E-Mail: info@jstmackintosh.co.uk

Keeble Hawson Moorhouse (Solicitors), Protection House,16-17 East Parade, Leeds, LS1 2BR, Mr H D McKillop, Tel: 0113 244 3121, E-Mail: postroom@keeblehawson.co.uk

Lawrence Tucketts, Bush House, 72 Prince Street, Bristol, BS99 7JZ, Mr. R M Staunton, Tel: 0117 9295295, E-Mail: robinstaunton@lawrence-tucketts.co.uk

Leathes Prior, 74 The Close, Norwich, Norfolk, NR1 4DR, Mr R J Chadd, Tel: 01603 610911, E-Mail: jc.leathes@btinternet.com

Levy & Macrae, 266 St Vincent Street, Glasgow, G2 5RL, Mr A Caplan, Tel: 0141 307 2311, E-Mail: tonycaplan@lamac.co.uk

Maclay Murray & Spens, 151 St Vincent Street, Glasgow, G2 5NJ, Ms M Burnside, Tel: 0141 2485011, E-Mail: mab@maclaymurrayspens.co.uk Web site: www.maclaymurrayspens.co.uk

Marshall Ross & Prevezer, 10-11 New Street, London, EC2M 4TP, Mr R Levitt, Solicitor & Trade Mark Attorney, Tel: 0171 626 1533, Mr J Cohen, Solicitor & Trade Mark Attorney, Tel: 0171 626 1533, E-Mail: prevezer@compuserve.com

Mundays, Crown Housel, Church Road, Claygate, Esher, KT10 OLP, Mr M Ishani, BFA Legal Committee, Tel: 01372 467272, E-Mail: hub@mundays.co.uk

Nina Moran-Watson, Solicitors, The Lodge House, Crow Lane, Tendring, Essex, CO16 9AP, Ms Nina Moran Watson, Tel: 01255 830045 mobile 07968 445804, E-Mail: nmoran-watson@btclick.com, home.btclick.com/nmoran-watson

Osborne Clarke, 50 Queen Charlotte Street, Bristol, BS1 4HE, Mr A Braithwaite, Tel: 0117 923 0220 , E-Mail: joanmckinney@osborne-clarke.com Web site: www.osborne-clarke.co.uk

Owen White, Senate House, 62-70 Bath Road, Slough, Berkshire, SL1 3SR, Mr. A Bates, Legal Advisor to the British Franchise Association, Tel: 01753 536846 E-Mail: anton.bates@owenwhite.com Web site: www.owenwhite.com

Parker Bullen, 45 Castle Street, Salisbury, Wilts, SP1 3SS, Mr M Lello, Tel: 01722 412000, Fax: 01722 411822, E-Mail: ParkerBull@aol.com

Paul K Nolan & Co., 135 Upper Lisburn Road, Belfast, BT10 OLH, Mr. P Nolan, Tel: 01232 301933, E-Mail: marie@pkn.co.uk

Paul K Nolan & Co., Merchants Hall, 25/26 Merchants Quay, Dublin 8, Ireland, Mr P Nolan, Tel: 01232 301933, E-Mail: marie@pkn.co.uk

Pinsent Curtis, 3 Colmore Circus, Birmingham, B4 6BH, Mr J Pratt, BFA Legal Committee, Tel: 0121 200 1050, E-Mail: john.pratt@pinsent-curtis.co.uk

Shadbolt & Co., Chatham Court, Lesbourne, Reigate, Surrey, RH2 7LD, Mr A J Trotter, Tel: 01737 226277, E-Mail: andrew_trotter@shadboltlaw.co.uk

Sherwin Oliver, New Hampshire Court, St Pauls Road, Portsmouth, PO5 4JT, Mr G Sturgess, Tel: 01705 832200, E-Mail: gsturgess@sherwin-oliver.co.uk Web site: www.british-franchise.org.uk/sherwin-oliver

Sylvester Amiel Lewin & Horne, Pearl Assurance House, 319 Ballards Lane, London, N12 8LY, Mr J Horne, Tel: 0181 446 4000, E-Mail: lawyers@sylvam.co.uk

Taylor Joynson Garrett, Carmelite, 50 Victoria Embankment, Blackfriars, London, EC4Y 0DX, Mr C Lloyd, Tel: 0171 353 1234, E-Mail: clloyd@tjg.co.uk

Thomas Eggar Church Adams, Fulwood House, Fulwood Place, London, WC1V 6HR, Mr. M Crooks, Tel: 0171 242 0841, E-Mail: mail@teca.demon.co.uk

Thomas Eggar Church Adams, Chatham Court, Lesbourne Road, Reigate, Surrey, RH2 7FN, Mr M Crooks, Tel: 01737 240111, E-Mail: michaelcrooks@teca.co.uk

Wragge & Co., 55 Colmore Row, Birmingham, B3 2AS, Mr G D Harris, Tel: 0121 233 1000, E-Mail: gordon_harris@wragge.com

Wright Johnston & Mackenzie, 12 St Vincent Place, Glasgow, G1 2EQ, Mr K McCracken, Tel: 0141 248 3434, E-Mail: enquiries@wjm.co.uk

TRAINING PROVIDERS

Franchise & Training Centre, 25 New Street Square, London, EC4A 3LN, Mr B Duckett, Tel: 0171 917 9824

The Franchise Training Centre, 212 Picadilly, London, W1V 9LD, Mr B Duckett, Tel: 0171 917 2837, E-Mail: franchising.uk@horwath.com

APPENDIX E: FRANCHISE EXHIBITIONS

The following list shows the franchising exhibitions that were scheduled for the year 2000. A similar pattern exists for most years and full details may be obtained from the BFA, including complete dates, contact numbers and websites.

January	Amsterdam, Netherlands; Vigo, Spain; Lausanne, Switzerland and the British Franchise Exhibition in Manchester
February	Adana, Turkey; San Diego, USA; Athens, Greece
March	Taipei, Taiwan; Brussels, Belgium; Paris, France; Sydney, Australia
April	Lisbon, Portugal; Dubai, UAE; Madrid, Spain; Syracuse, Italy; Taipei, Taiwan; and the British and International Franchise Exhibition at Wembley, London
May	Bari, Italy; Orlando, USA; Rome, Italy; Amsterdam, Netherlands
June	Sofia, Bulgaria; Sao Paulo, Brazil; Frankfurt am Main, Germany
August	Kuala Lumpur, Maylasia
September	Singapore; UK National Franchise Week, Birmingham
October	Melbourne, Australia; Budapest, Hungary; Valencia, Spain; Vienna, Austria; Copenhagen, Denmark
November	Manila, Philippines; Beijing, China; Guangzhou, China; Milan, Italy; Shanghai, China

For information on the UK exhibitions, including lists of exhibitors, visit www.franinfo.co.uk

APPENDIX F: FRANCHISE PUBLICATIONS

MAGAZINES

Business Franchise. The official journal of the British Franchise Association, published 10 times a year by Miller Freeman UK, 630 Chiswick High Road, London, W4 5BG. Tel: 0208 742 2828

The definitive information source covering financial and legal advice, marketing and company profiles.

Target readership: Anyone looking to buy a franchise or to franchise their business.

The same source also publishes the British Franchise Directory

Franchise World. Published on alternate months by and supplied direct from Franchise World, James House, 37 Nottingham Road, London SW17 7EA. Tel: 0208 767 1371.

Up-to-date news on franchise launches, reports of current opportunities and features by franchise specialists in accountancy, banking, law and management make this an informative and invaluable magazine. Contains a full coverage of the franchise scene from the perspective of both the franchisee and franchisor.

The same source also publishes the Franchise World Directory

The Franchise Magazine. Published on alternate months by and available from Franchise Development Services, 56 Surrey Street, Norwich, Norfolk NR1 3FD. Tel: 01603 620301.

This magazine introduces you to the world of franchising and new business opportunities. Editorials, articles, news items, statistics, financial and legislative changes and reviews create a compelling read.

Target readership: Individuals and organisations seeking to own and operate their own business under the franchise system. Also targeted to business to business providers interested in the continued growth markets that franchising offers.

Franchise International. Published quarterly by and available from Franchise Development Services, 56 Surrey Street, Norwich, Norfolk NR1 3FD. Tel: 01603 620301. Features, news and advice on export and import of franchise systems.

Target readership: Individuals and organisations worldwide seeking major franchise investment and development opportunities with a minimum capital availability of $500,000.

The same source also publishes the UK Franchise Directory

DIRECTORIES

Business Franchise Directory. Published annually by Miller Freeman UK, 630 Chiswick High Road, London, W4 5BG. Tel: 0208 742 2828. Includes financial and legal advice from leading experts and lists all available franchises in he UK.

Franchise World Directory. Published annually by and supplied direct from Franchise World, James House, 37 Nottingham Road, London SW17 7EA. Tel: 0208 767 1371.

Large and reliable, with bi-monthly updates in Franchise World magazine. A very comprehensive list of franchises are detailed – contact names, start-up costs, sales and profit levels, growth rates, etc – in 12 major categories. There are also useful articles written by franchise experts.

The United Kingdom Franchise Directory. Published annually by and obtainable from Franchise Development Services, 56 Surrey Street, Norwich, Norfolk NR1 3FD. Tel: 01603 620301.

Hugely popular, listing every British franchisor trading, including type of business, number of franchise operations, investment needed, royalties payable etc. Additional features are well worth reading, too.

These books, directories and magazines may be stocked by your local library.

APPENDIX G: USEFUL CONTACTS

ACCOUNTANTS

Institute of Chartered Accountants (England and Wales), Chartered Accountants Hall, PO Box 433, Moorgate Place, London EC2R 6EQ. Tel: 0207 920 8100

Institute of Chartered Accountants of Scotland, 27 Queen Street, Edinburgh EH2 ILA, Tel: 0131 225 5673

Institute of Chartered Accountants in Ireland, Chartered Accountants House, 87-89 Pembroke Road, Dublin 4. Tel: 0001 680400

Chartered Association of Certified Accountants, 29 Lincolns Inn Fields, London WC2A 3EE. Tel: 0207 242 6855

CHAMBERS OF COMMERCE/TRADE

British Chambers of Commerce, 4 Westwood House, Westwood Business Park, Coventry, Warwickshire, CV4 8HS, tel: 01203 694484

ENTERPRISE AGENCIES

Business in the Community, 44 Baker Street, London, W1M 1DH, Tel: 0207 224 1600

ESTATE AGENTS

Incorporated Society of Valuers and Auctioneers, 3 Cadogan Gate, London SWIX OAS, Tel: 0207 235 2282

National Association of Estate Agents, 21 Jury Street, Warwick, Warwickshire CV34 4EH, Tel: 01926 496800

INSURANCE BROKERS

The British Insurance and Investment Brokers Association, 14 Bevis Marks, London, EC3A 7NT, Tel: 0207 623 9043

PRODUCT PROTECTION ORGANISATIONS

The Chartered Institute of Patent Agents, Staple Inn Buildings, High Holborn, London, WCIV 7PZ, Tel: 0207 405 9450

The Institute of Trade Mark Agents, Canterbury House, 2-6 Sydenham Road, Croydon, Surrey CR0 9XE, Tel: 0181 686 2052

The Patent Office, The Design Registry and The Registrar of Trademarks, State House, 66-71 High Holborn, London WCIR 4TP, Tel: 0645 500505

RESEARCH ORGANISATIONS

The Department of Enterprise, Trade and Investment, IDB House, 64 Chichester Street, Belfast BT1 4JX. Tel: 02890 234488. This is where the Companies Registration Office is located in Northern Ireland.

Financial Times Research Centre, Tabernacle Court, 16-28 Tabernacle Street, London EC2A 4DD, Tel: 0207 970 0100

Jordan's Business Information Service, Jordan House, 21 St Thomas Street, Bristol, BS1 6JS, Tel: 01179 230600

Mintel International Ltd, 18-19 Long Lane, London, ECIA 9HE, Tel: 0207 606 4533

The Registrar of Companies (UK), Companies House, Crown Way, Maindy, Cardiff, CF14 3UZ,. Tel: 01222 380801

SMALL BUSINESS ASSOCIATIONS

The Highlands and Islands Development Board, Bridge House, 20 Bridge Street, Inverness IV1 IQR, Tel: 01463 234171

Northern Ireland Development Board, The Local Enterprise Development Unit, Lamont House, Purdys Lane, Belfast BT8, Tel: 02890 232755

Development Board for Rural Wales, Ladywell House, Newtown, Powys SY16 IJB. Tel: 01686 626965

National Federation of Self-Employed and Small Businesses, Whittle Way, Blackpool Business Park, Blackpool, Lancs., SY4 2FE, Tel: 01253 336000

The Rural Development Commission, 11 Cowley Street, London SWIP 3NA. Tel: 0207 276 6969

Scottish Enterprise, 120 Bothwell Street, Glasgow G2 7PJ. Tel: 0141 248 2700

SMALL FIRMS SERVICE

Small Firms Centres (Freephone 2444) will put you in touch with your nearest Small Firms Centre.

SURVEYORS

The Royal Institution of Chartered Surveyors, 12 Great George Street, London SWIP 3AD, Tel: 0171 222 7000

INDEX